The Boy Rover, or the Smuggler of the South Seas. [By Lieut. Parker, pseud.]

Anonymous, Lieutenant Parker

The BiblioLife Network

This project was made possible in part by the BiblioLife Network (BLN), a project aimed at addressing some of the huge challenges facing book preservationists around the world. The BLN includes libraries, library networks, archives, subject matter experts, online communities and library service providers. We believe every book ever published should be available as a high-quality print reproduction; printed on- demand anywhere in the world. This insures the ongoing accessibility of the content and helps generate sustainable revenue for the libraries and organizations that work to preserve these important materials.

The following book is in the "public domain" and represents an authentic reproduction of the text as printed by the original publisher. While we have attempted to accurately maintain the integrity of the original work, there are sometimes problems with the original book or micro-film from which the books were digitized. This can result in minor errors in reproduction. Possible imperfections include missing and blurred pages, poor pictures, markings and other reproduction issues beyond our control. Because this work is culturally important, we have made it available as part of our commitment to protecting, preserving, and promoting the world's literature.

GUIDE TO FOLD-OUTS, MAPS and OVERSIZED IMAGES

In an online database, page images do not need to conform to the size restrictions found in a printed book. When converting these images back into a printed bound book, the page sizes are standardized in ways that maintain the detail of the original. For large images, such as fold-out maps, the original page image is split into two or more pages.

Guidelines used to determine the split of oversize pages:

• Some images are split vertically; large images require vertical and horizontal splits.
• For horizontal splits, the content is split left to right.
• For vertical splits, the content is split from top to bottom.
• For both vertical and horizontal splits, the image is processed from top left to bottom right.

ROVER

OR

THE SMUGGLER OF THE SOUTH SEAS

THE BOY ROVER;

OR,

THE SMUGGLER OF THE SOUTH SEAS.

THE MAIDEN ON THE ROCK.

CHAPTER I.

THE STORM—THE WATCHER—THE FALSE LIGHT—
THE DOOMED SHIP.

IT was night—night upon the ocean—and dark clouds hung like a funeral pall upon all around.

The day had been fair and bright, but the coming darkness had given unmistakeable tokens of approaching storm.

Dark clouds were rising and gathering, and the atmosphere was sultry and oppressive.

In the distance the low rumbling thunder was breaking through the clouds, and echoing from wave to cliff.

The sea was rising, and the waves were crested with a white sparkling foam.

The lightning played in the heavens, and ever and anon cast its lurid glare across the reeking waters.

It was a terrible night, and ashore the prayers of the inhabitants of the coast were offered for the souls of the poor mariners at sea.

On a steep cliff, overhanging the shingly beach, on which the waves were now breaking with mad fury and throwing their foam-bespangled crests, sat a lad of some seventeen summers, peering out into the far-off darkness of the ocean.

Motionless as a corpse, his hand shading his eyes, and his thin lips compressed tightly together, there he sat gazing steadfastly over the waters.

An hour had passed since he had first taken up his present position, but not for one moment had he taken his gaze from the spot on which he looked.

Still the storm-clouds gathered, and higher and higher dashed the waves upon the beach.

The lightning became more vivid, and the thunder louder in its intensity—large drops of rain fell; yet still, motionless as a statue, sat the eager watcher.

Suddenly a bright flash of forked-lightning lit up the foaming ocean, and the boy started to his feet.

"At last," he exclaimed, "my patience has been rewarded!"

With one bound he leaped from the cliff, and disappeared in the darkness.

The storm now burst forth with redoubled fury. Flash followed flash—lighting up the foam-crested billows with a phosphorescent glare—and the thunder rolled away in the distance like salvos of artillery.

It was a fearful night, and woe to the vessel that should lose her course, and approach those dangerous rocks.

For the waves dashed upon them in mad fury; and strength and skill would prove of no avail in contest with their powers.

A bright light now shone forth over the waves, and in the far off distance the white sails of a vessel were plainly discernible.

Her course was set fair for the rock-bound shore,

They had seen the beacon, and now steered their course direct for their expected haven of refuge.

But all is not gold that glitters; and the hand extended in welcome oft hides the dagger in the sleeve.

On came the fated bark, ploughing the angry waves like a thing of life.

But the storm was fast gathering in fury, and the captain saw, with the eye of an experienced mariner, the danger that threatened them.

It was, therefore, with a gladdened heart that he saw the bright light shining over the sea.

And the passengers hearts beat in unison with his own.

On steered the tight little craft towards the now brilliant beacon; and on, fiercer and fiercer, raged the storm.

Every sail was reefed close—not a stitch of canvass was left exposed for the wind to lay hold of—and, with anxious mien, the captain paced the deck, giving his orders in a cool collected manner.

"Breakers ahead!" suddenly rang out from the mast-head.

"Where! away?" shouted the captain.

"On the larboard-bow" was the response.

"Helm a port!" shouted the captain.

There was a breathless suspense for a moment; and then the voice of the helmsman rang out, clear and loud—

"She will not answer her helm."

"Breakers ahead!" rang out again, clear and loud, from the mast-head. "Helm a port!—helm a port!—or we are lost!"

For a moment—and a moment only—the captain stood irresolute; then, grasping his glass and springing into the rigging, he surveyed the surrounding coast.

Long and anxious was his gaze; his face paled, and his limbs trembled, but not a word or act betrayed his fears. Leaping to her deck, he exclaimed: "Stand by with the hatchets to clear her! Men, to your duty!"

There was an awful suspense as the brave ship rushed madly on to her doom.

"Lighten her," exclaimed the captain; "throw everything overboard that can ease her!"

"Ay, ay, sir," was the immediate response.

"Now she rides more easy," said the captain, as one by one the casks and bales fell over her side.

"'Bout ship!" again commanded Captain Walters. "More hands at the tiller!"

Three or four men rushed up to assist the helmsman; but all in vain were their endeavours to ease her off the coast.

The first mate now approached to where the captain stood, and, placing his hand to his cap, remarked—

"Captain, I fear yon light has deceived us."

"How, sir?" asked his superior.

"I cannot help thinking that is a wrecker's beacon, luring us to destruction."

"By heaven such a suspicion but now crossed my mind, as I perceived, by the lightning's flash, the long line of breakers on our larboard bow."

"And we are drifting towards them, sir, with a speed which threatens the destruction of our brave little craft, and every soul on board her."

"We will place our faith in Providence, Mr. Murray. The wind may yet change, and bear us out seaward."

"It may!" was the laconic reply.

But Mr. Murray was too old a sailor to believe it; and Captain Walters had dared the dangerous waves too long not to doubt even his own remark. Too well he knew the danger to which his vessel was exposed, and the fate which awaited his crew and passengers, when once within that line of foaming breakers.

Still on she went, her bows pointed direct to the seething foam; and the cheeks of the brave seamen paled as each succeeding flash showed the white line of breakers nearer and nearer to their devoted vessel.

And the passengers clung to each other in terror, and murmured a prayer to heaven for their safety.

"Hold on, for your lives!" exclaimed the captain, as a bright flash of lightning lit up the sea for a moment, and revealed the dreadful breakers close under her bows.

"Hold on, and stand firm!" echoed the mate, "or, by heavens, we are food for fishes!"

Scarce had the words passed his lips than the fated bark was lifted, as it were, by giant hands, high up on the crested waves, and then hurled wildly down into the vortex of the foaming water.

Every plank of the gallant little bark creaked

and groaned, as though in agony at the fearful strain upon her timbers, and every joint started and gaped.

Up again she rose, and down again, with mad fury, she plunged, whilst her beams creaked, and her joints gaped wider and wider.

The foaming waves dashed madly over her decks. and, with a thundering sound, swept back into the angry sea, carrying with them every article in their course.

Frantically did the crew and passengers of that doomed ship hold on to the rigging; for so fearful was the violence of the waves that they literally tore portions of the clothing from their persons, as they rushed back into the surging waste.

Up again she rose, and for a moment steadied herself on the bosom of the waves.

"Get all ready," exclaimed the captain, "to lower the boats. Though heaven knows," he added, in a low tone, to his inferior officer, "nothing can live in such a sea as this."

"Ay, ay, sir," said an old salt, and several of the seamen instantly set about the work.

But scarce had they commenced their task when a high wave swept her decks, and carried three of the men over her sides.

A loud cry for help rose above the howling of the storm; but all on board that craft were powerless to aid them.

The angry waves dashed them forward towards the beach, and the thunder roared the requiem of three as brave fellows as ever sailed the salt waters.

On drifted the ship, into the line of foam. Up high on the crested waves she rose—then down into the valley of waters — creaking, groaning, careering, rolling, like a thing of life in agony — whilst the now pale-faced trembling crew clung to every available rope in horror and dismay.

All chance of saving her was now lost. Not a soul on board that fated ship but now saw plainly that she must be dashed to pieces; and, in the frenzy of despair, they cast their eyes eagerly around for any article that would serve to support them in the water.

The waves tore over her decks, and the water poured through her joints. Again she was lifted high up; and then, with the speed of an arrow, down she went.

There was a fearful crash—a wild piercing shriek from the women, a cry of horror from the men—and the main-mast fell, carrying with it many of its living freight over the side.

"Cut away!" exclaimed Captain Walters— "strike for your lives, men—strike!"

The sailors brought their hatchets down with fearful force upon the cordage, and in a few moments the mast went over her sides.

The vessel shivered and shook, then righted herself for a moment. But it was for a moment only, for down again she went upon the rocks, crushing in her timbers with a fearful shock, and she careered over on her side.

The waves swept over her decks, and, as one long, agonised, piercing shriek rose from that ill-fated craft, with a gurgling sound she parted amidships, and sunk in the wild foaming waters that lashed that rock-bound shore.

Down she went, whilst the lightning flashed, as though in mockery at her fate and the foam-crested waves leaped and sported around her, forming a winding-sheet for those who, a few short hours before, were full of life and hopes.

CHAPTER II

THE SECRET CAVERN—THE MURDER ON THE ROCKS—THE CURSE.

WHEN the young watcher, whom we saw seated on the cliff, had disappeared from the rocks, he hurried on a distance of some hundred yards, when, taking a small tube from his pocket, he placed it to his lips, and blew a shrill sharp whistle.

In a moment another whistle answered his own, and a form, which seemed to arise from the ground, suddenly stood by his side.

"There is work to-night for the boys," he said, addressing the new comer. "The beacon must be lighted, and all hands turn out."

"All right, captain," remarked the other; "it will put them in good spirits."

And, as he spoke, he disappeared as mysteriously as he came, in the darkness.

For a moment the other stood gazing around him, and appeared to listen eagerly; then he muttered to himself—

"Another ship doomed: more souls to perish; more homes to be made desolate! Psha!—away with all qualms of conscience! Let them die. There is music in their groans. My oath is registered, and it shall be kept. My hand shall be at the throat of all. I have sworn it, and I will keep my oath."

A bright flash of lightning at this moment lit up the spot on which he stood, and revealed an opening at his feet.

This he descended into, and, stooping low, passed through a dark passage some twenty feet in length; and from thence into a large cave, which was dimly lighted by an oil lamp that swung from the roof.

In this cavern, which Nature herself had formed in the rocks, and which was only known to its present occupants, were several persons — all young — not one exceeding the age of twenty years; but a more determined-looking set of fellows could seldom or ever be met with at a time.

Their costume was principally that of fishermen, or persons engaged about the coast; but their occupation, we shall see, was anything but that which is known by the word "honourable."

He who had watched upon the cliff approached to the centre of the cave, and, as the light of the lamp fell upon his features, revealed a face deathly pale, a forehead high, and smoothed as polished marble. But there was an expression about the eyes and mouth that denoted a firm resolve and an unflinching courage. He was tall and well-built, and his limbs bore that sinewy development seldom seen among those to whom fresh air and healthy exercise are things to be coveted, but rarely possessed.

There was something, too, commanding in his tones, as he addressed those assembled in that out-of-the-world place.

"Throw open the port-hole," he exclaimed, "and fire the beacon."

In an instant several stout boards, rudely but firmly joined together, and bedaubed so as to resemble as much as possible the stone, were drawn aside, and revealed an opening in the cavern.

Before this opening several busy hands placed a quantity of wood, and then poured over it some oil

"Light up?" said one, addressing him we have described.

"At once," was the reply—"and to your different stations."

"Ay, ay," was the only remark to this.

In another moment the fire was burning brightly, and throwing a lurid glare over the waves, which could be seen rolling in their fury on the beach.

One by one the occupants of that subterranean retreat passed through the passage, and out into the open air.

Not a word was spoken, and each took his way in a different direction.

He who had been called "captain" was left alone.

When the echoes of the last footstep had died away, he approached the opening, and looked forth upon the sea.

For some moments he gazed intently upon the rolling billows, as they danced and leaped in the glare of the fire-light. Then he muttered—

"How wild and furious is this scene—wild as my own heart! There is music, too, in those foaming waters, that sends the life-blood coursing through my veins. It was such a night as this when he left us—when his cruel hand struck her to the earth! But she shall be avenged—ay, though seas divide us, and a life-time is spent in its consummation!"

Still far over the waters his gaze was fixed, as though there he would find the subject that lay at his heart, when a loud crash of thunder seemed to break the reverie into which he had fallen, for he started suddenly round, and walked hastily towards the passage.

Then as suddenly he halted, and, taking a long Spanish clasp-knife from his pocket, opened the blade, and placed the weapon in his belt.

Once more casting his eyes around the apartment, he strode from the cave, and again made for the rock where he had been so intently watching a short time before.

The vessel was now rapidly nearing the breakers, and, seating himself in the same position he had before occupied, he watched intently the doomed ship.

Not a muscle of his face moved—not a word of hope or fear for its safety escaped him—as he saw her nearing those dangerous rocks.

But when she struck, his eye brightened, and he leaped to his feet.

But not with the intention of rendering aid—no, his mission there was not mercy.

For the passions of hell were in his heart, and his soul was filled with blood.

So young—so noble in his mien—so base, so hellish in his thoughts!

The generous qualities of manhood were eradicated from his breast, and he was actuated but by one thought—revenge.

On whom, and for what, time will show.

Scarce had the echoes of those fearful shrieks died away in the storm, when he perceived, by the light of the false beacon, several forms being hurled towards the rock on which he stood.

Plainly he could distinguish a man bearing on one arm the form of a young female, whilst with the other he buffetted the fierce waves.

Vainly he strove to save her from being dashed to pieces. A huge wave rolled in, and carried them some distance up the rock.

As it receded, the stout swimmer caught hold of a projection of the stone, and succeeded, at the sacrifice of lacerated hands, in preventing himself and companion from being carried back into the surging waters.

But here he seemed powerless to move, and, with his insensible burden, sank exhausted.

The watcher now descended from his position to the ledge of the rock on which the shipwrecked beings lay.

Intently he gazed upon them for a moment, and then, stooping down, placed his hand upon the breast of the exhausted man.

Did he seek to know if he still lived? No; his hand strayed not to ascertain the pulsation of the heart; but to discover if wealth were concealed there.

He thrust his hand into the bosom of the man's shirt, and drew forth a small canvass bag.

The shipwrecked man started to his feet as the other was about to secrete his booty about his own person.

"Villain!" he exclaimed, as he grasped the throat of the young captain. "Is your heart so callous that you can rob a man in my position?"

So sudden was the attack that for a moment the youth was staggered; but the next instant the long Spanish knife was raised above his head, and then buried up to its handle in the bosom of the shipwrecked mariner.

The hot blood spurted up over his hand, and the grasp on his throat relaxed.

"The curse of a dying man," exclaimed the sailor, "pursue you through life! Sleeping and waking may you never more know peace! May you live in misery and die in despair!"

His head fell back. He was dead; and the young murderer thrust him over the rock into the foaming billows.

CHAPTER III.

THE LOVERS—THE ROPE.

When the ill-fated ship went to pieces amid the breakers, the most fearful confusion prevailed among the panic-stricken souls who so short a time before had looked forward with fond hope and expectation to the meeting of friends so dear to them; and the thought of the kind words and cheerful smiles which would greet them after their long absence from their native land, had cheered the dreary voyage, and made their hearts light and buoyant.

But, alas! how oft are we doomed to disappointment when our fond desires are about to be realised; how oft the black clouds of adversity throw their dark shadow across the sunshine of joy!

Many a heart that beat high with pleasure now lie still and cold, never more to throb; and many an eye that gazed anxiously across the sea, to catch the first glimpse of the white cliffs of Old Albion, now was glazed and stony in the embrace of death!

To them the joys and sorrows of this world were nought; their souls had winged their flight to eternity.

Out of forty-four souls, who a short time before were full of life and health, but three had escaped Death's keen scythe.

Dashed to pieces upon the rocks, or washed out to sea by the receding waves, they had sunk beneath the billows, never more to rise.

We have seen how the brave sailor, after buffetting the furious waves, succeeded in landing his fair burden on the rock; but we have yet to follow the fortunes of another, who, when the ship struck, was carried overboard by the shock, and succeeded in grasping a portion of the wreck, which buoyed him up upon the bosom of those furious waters.

Ere the shades of evening had closed in, he had stood upon the deck, gazing towards the shore, with hope and love in his breast; his arm was encircling the waist of a fair girl, whom he was conducting to that home where the sunlight of her smile, and her innocent and loving nature, were to shed a halo of love and peace.

But the clouds gathered, and the storm burst forth, and the first shadow was cast upon their happiness.

He had stood by her side during those fearful moments, and she had clung to his bosom for help and safety.

But the fearful crash, when the keel struck upon the rocks, had severed their frantic embrace, and, as the vessel lurched over, they were precipitated at the same moment into the boiling waves.

Each in their horror uttered the other's name; but the angry winds carried their tones far away, and the roaring waters hissed their voices to scorn.

And the cruel waters bore them rapidly from each other. The poor girl closed her eyes, and breathed a prayer to heaven. She was fast sinking under the waves, and insensibility was stealing over her soul; but a strong arm grasped her fragile form, and she was hurried away as the waters faded from her sight.

But he, bearing upon his frail support, breasted the raging billows with a strength and determination that showed he would struggle on whilst he had life.

It was not the frenzy of despair; but the determination to live for himself and for her.

"While there is life there is hope," he thought, as he strained his eyes to penetrate the darkness, in the hope of seeing that loved form.

But it was hope against hope.

The shadows were too dense; he could see nothing but the white-crested waves, and the now fast-fading beacon that had lured them to their doom.

With a groan of agony he struck out manfully for that light, and, with a prayer to heaven for the safety of her he sought in vain, he laid his breast upon the friendly timber, and swam with long and rapid strokes.

The spray dashed in his face and half-blinded him, and the force of the waves nearly deprived him of his breath. But still he battled on.

The light drew nearer and nearer, though fainter and fainter in its brilliancy.

He found that he was upon the rocks, and he drew himself up to save being dashed to pieces on them.

A huge wave rolled in, and threw him forward. He stretched forth his hand to save his skull from being split by the mass of stone before him. As he did so, his friendly raft slipped from beneath him, and his hand came in contact with a rope.

This he grasped firmly, and the receding wave left him dangling by his hand in the air

So close was he to the fire-beacon that its warmth almost scorched his face.

But the rope! The thought instantly took possession of his mind that it had been thrown by some friendly hand.

He found that his exertions in the water had almost exhausted his strength, for his arms would scarce bear the weight of his body.

But to hang there was to enhance his weakness; to drop might cause him to fracture his limbs; or he might be carried out by the next wave: he therefore determined to climb the rope.

But this was a task of some difficulty, so weak had he become.

He put forth all the strength he could muster, and ascended. When he had got some few yards up, he placed his foot upon the rock to take breath, and, to his surprise, found the ledge sufficiently wide to stand upon. He looked round, gazed intently at the fire, and saw that it was at the mouth of an opening in the rock.

With a thankful heart, he once more grasped the rope firmly in his hands, and drew himself upwards to a level with the opening. Then, swinging himself forward, landed himself in the opening, beside the burning embers.

He saw there was a large open space beyond, and he rushed forward; but here his strength gave way, and he sank exhausted upon the floor of the cavern.

And there he lay for several minutes, scarcely able to realise his situation—his hair matted on his temples his clothes clinging tightly to his limbs, and striking a chilling numbness to his weary frame.

His mind, too, was paralysed, and his brain bewildered; and it was not till a loud clap of thunder reverberated through the cave that he aroused himself from the lethargic stupor into which he had fallen, and started hurriedly to his feet.

With surprise and astonishment he gazed around him.

"Where am I?" he wondered. "What place can this be?"

Then he looked again and again at the various things the cave contained.

And it was filled indeed with a heterogenous mass. Barrels, chests, cordage, and articles of all descriptions met his sight

He walked from one end of the cavern to the other. Yet go which way he would, still he saw nothing but piles of goods. It resembled the warehouse of a ship-chandler; for most every article that he saw was appertaining to furnishing of ships.

He looked in vain for some one to solve the mystery. But not a living being encountered his sight. Yet there was unmistakeable evidence of human life about the place.

On a huge board, which was placed across several barrels, in the centre of the cave, were cans, drinking-horns, pipes, and all the evidences of several persons having but recently been regaling themselves. But where were they now?

He once more approached the opening where the fire, now but a few smouldering ashes, had lured the fated ship to her doom. He looked out upon the tossing waves for a moment; then turned again, with a heavy heart to the cave.

As he did so, his eye caught the glare of a polished sheet of metal, which was placed in a slanting direction above his head. It was placed there as a reflector, and it had reflected the light of those treacherous embers over the waves.

Then he started, and a cold shiver ran through his frame.

"Heavens! I see it all now," he exclaimed, aloud. "This fire is a wrecker's light, and this a wrecker's cave. They have lured us upon this treacherous coast; they have sacrificed us to their accursed longing for plunder. Oh, I see it all now. I see it all!"

He paused, irresolute, for a moment; and then,

dashing the wet locks from his forehead, he almost hissed between his teeth, in agonised tones

"Curse them for their hellish work! Oh, that earth can produce such wretches to sacrifice innocent lives to their fiendish lust for gain. And Ellen—my poor loved Ellen - to meet such a fate through the instrumentality of these fiends!"

He buried his face in his hands, in an agony of grief and despair.

But not long thus did he remain, for, raising his head, he muttered—

"But I know their haunt! Providence has made me the instrument of their detection, and Justice shall meet them out their reward. Yes, I know their haunt the means by which they lure so many souls to destruction! Though the waves roll mountains high, I will again breast them, that I may bring the blood-hounds of the law upon their track! Oh, Ellen, you shall be avenged—terribly avenged."

He turned again to the opening, and stretched forth his hand to clutch the rope by which he ascended, with the firm resolve of again daring the waves, and endeavouring to swim to some portion of the coast where he might obtain assistance to secure those whom he believed had been the cause of his present misery. But the rope was gone!

'Twas well for him that it was so; for, in his desperate mood, he would have rushed upon his destruction.

He gazed down upon the dashing spray; he saw that the leap would be madness, and, with clenched hands and firm-set teeth, he strode to the centre of the cave.

He listened intently; not a human sound broke the silence.

"I have escaped a watery grave," he thought, "perhaps to meet a worse fate; for, should I be discovered, they will doubtless slay me, for I know their secret haunt, and would betray them. Aye, they would slay me; for well they know that dead men tell no tales. They may shortly return with anything they may pick up from the wreck; I must endeavour to conceal myself, and wait some opportunity to escape from here. Oh, would that I had some weapon with which to defend myself; and I would sell my life dearly."

He looked anxiously around, in the hope of possessing himself with some means of defence; but nothing caught his eye.

Against the side of the cavern was a large seaman's chest; he walked towards it, and raised the lid.

He started with joy, for it contained a pair of pistols, a powder-flask, and several articles of clothing.

To possess himself of the weapons and flask was the work of a moment; and, as he was about to examine them, he heard the voices of men in conversation.

To close the lid of the box, and seek some place of concealment, rushed across his mind; but where, where to hide?

He could see no place where he was not likely to be discovered. A pleased expression broke over his face.

Advancing to the rude table, he raised one end of the board; the casks upon which it stood were empty, and minus their tops.

"This is my only chance," he muttered; "but any port in a storm."

And as the voices sounded louder and nearer, he lifted the board high enough to give him a passage, and drew himself over the edge of the

cask, and lowered himself into its interior. Then, easing the board steadily down again into its place, he crouched into a painful attitude, and listened intently.

Scarce had he done so, when two men, staggering under a couple of heavy bales, entered the cavern.

"I'm blowed, Bill, if it ain't nearly broke my back!" exclaimed one, addressing his companion. "No little weight, and I'm cursed glad to get rid of it."

And so saying, he let it drop from his shoulders on to the table.

"That makes two," exclaimed the other, with a grin, as he placed another bale beside its companion on the table. "This will be a good night's work, for the shore is covered with them. So come on; no skulking!"

And, with an oath, they left the cavern.

The hidden youth heard all that passed, and the blood almost stagnated at his heart as he heard the bales fall upon the board above his head. His heart sunk within him. He put forth all his strength to raise it, but was powerless to move it one inch; he felt that he was indeed doomed, and he leant back against the side of the cask in an agony of despair.

———

CHAPTER IV.

THE MURDERER AND HIS CAPTIVE—THE ATTEMPTED OUTRAGE—AN UNLOOKED-FOR DELIVERANCE.

LET us now return to the youthful murderer on the rock, and the poor girl who lay insensible at his feet.

When Mr. Murray, the mate of the vessel which had gone to pieces on the rocks (for he it was whose strong arms had borne the fair girl through the waves), had disappeared over the cliff into the boiling surf, the young man coolly wiped the bloody knife upon his sleeve, and replaced it in his belt; then, stooping down, he lifted the head of Ellen upon his knee, and peered into her face.

The flashes of lightning, which still continued in quick succession, revealed to his gaze the features of a damsel of some eighteen years of age, and of surpassing beauty, though the pallor of death was now upon her face, and her long glossy black curls hung wildly and matted over a neck and bosom of voluptuous symmetry.

There was a fiendish gleam in the eyes of the youth as his ravished gaze feasted upon the inanimate form of that poor girl.

And there was a demon in his heart, urging on his base passions to more unholy deeds.

He raised her, and, grasping her firmly in his strong arms, ascended to his former position.

But, powerful as he was, this was no easy task. He accomplished it, however; and after resting a moment, commenced descending on the other side, and made his way towards the cavern.

So still did she lie in his arms, that but for the gentle rise and fall of her bosom he would have thought she was dead.

Having arrived at the entrance of the cave, he gently lowered his burden down, descended himself, then half carried and half drew her along the passage and into the cave.

Here he placed her upon the large chest out of which her lover, a few minutes before, had abstracted the pistols to defend himself in case of need. Then, seating himself on a cask, which stood in close proximity to the chest, he awaited her recovery.

But her late horrible adventure had so prostrated her faculties, that it seemed she would never recover them.

After a few moments, he descended from his seat and approached the board. He selected a small flask from among the various articles, and, returning to the side of the insensible girl, placed it to her lips, and poured a portion of its contents into her mouth. He watched eagerly its effects; but still there were no signs of returning animation.

Again he applied the flask; but still the same effect.

"She had better sleep, perhaps," he muttered to himself; "she will recover soon enough to know her doom."

And walking to another part of the cavern, he drew another chest to the side of the one on which Ellen reclined; then, selecting some portions of sailcloth, he rolled one piece up, into a kind of pillow, and, lifting the girl from her seat, threw them over the boxes, and laid her down upon them; placing the piece he had rolled up under her head. This business accomplished, he took a deep draught from the flask, and walked towards the opening which looked out upon the sea.

Kicking the remains of the fire out of the opening into the beach, he seized the wooden partition and drew it back into its place; and the cave now presented no appearance of having the least outlet.

"It won't do her much good," he thought, "sleeping in her wet clothes in such a place as this; but she shall have dry ones ere long; aye, and a softer bed, too; that couch is too hard for her tender flesh."

And seating himself at the table, he waited impatiently the return of his followers.

It was not long before two came in, each bearing some article washed ashore from the wreck.

Their eyes immediately rested upon the form of Ellen as she lie motionless upon her rude couch, and a smile lit up their rude features as they turned enquiringly towards their leader.

"My eye, captain, she's a spanker!" exclaimed a broad-shouldered bull-headed fellow of twenty years of age. "Enough to make a fellow's mouth water to look at."

"Yer'd better mind what you're a saying," remarked the other, "or maybe, the captain will make your eyes water, if you make any remark till your turn comes."

"Well, that won't be long, Jim, I reckon, for the captain soon gets over his lot. Then comes Black Bill's, then Tom's, then mine."

"Silence!" exclaimed the captain, in a commanding tone. "No more of this foolery. Your turns will come in good time; but till then remember our compact. Ned Wilton, any news from the schooner?"

"None captain."

"All's right on board then? No cutter attempted to overhaul her, I suppose?"

"No; but Black Bill says he fancies there's one on the look-out."

"I've heard as much; and, as all her cargo's landed safely, I'll go abroad to-morrow, and we'll have another run."

"Well, if we can only keep it up for a year or two," said Jim, "that and the wrecker business together, we shall all be able to retire and live like gentleman for the rest of our lives. Happy and glorious!"

"Happy!" echoed the captain.

But the word seemed to die on his lips, and his brow contracted.

Several more of the wreckers now entered, all loaded like their predecessors. Each cast a furtive glance at the poor girl, and then at the captain; but the frowns that greeted their looks warned them to hazard no remark; so, divesting themselves of their various burdens, they sat about the cave in different attitudes.

When all had returned, the captain rose from his seat, and, after commanding attention, said—

"Now, lads, I have to tell you that I think it will be wiser to put to sea. I have heard enough to-day to convince me that the cutters are on the alert. We have hitherto succeeded in cheating the revenue of its due; I hope we shall be able to do so for some time to come. Our retreat is not likely to be discovered if we are not seen in the vicinity; and I do not think there is a traitor amongst us who would tell the secret. Nay, I am sure there is not; for it would not be worth while, as there is not one of us but is a branded felon. There lies our greatest security; for each has a hold upon his fellow, and the law has a hold upon us all. Besides, I have a another motive than business in once more putting to sea. Therefore, you will all at once take your departure for the schooner, except Jim and Ned, who will remain here on guard, and they, together with myself and yon maiden, will embark in the morning. Tell Black Bill to have everything in readiness for a cruise, and that nothing will remain but to weigh anchor and bid farewell for a time to the shores of Old England; and likewise tell him to see that Wild Madge has the cabin prepared for a lady-passenger. That is all I have to say till I rejoin you in the morning."

Without a word, all there assembled, save Ned and Jim, left the cave, and started for their mission. These two worthies stood awaiting any further orders of their leaders.

"You, Ned," said the captain, "after a time, will see that all is secure before our departure, lest any curious person should pry into our warehouse; but, for the present, one of you will keep guard at the entrance to the passage, the other at the coast. Should I need your presence, you will know the signals. To your posts!"

"Aye, aye, captain!" replied both the men, as they departed, Jim poking his tongue in his cheek, and twisting his eye round at his companion with a comical leer.

Ned dug his elbow into the ribs of his mate, as a sort of acknowledgement that he perfectly understood the other's meaning.

When the last echo of their footsteps had died away, the youthful captain again rose from his seat, and approached to the side of the insensible girl.

He leant over the rigid form, and gazed intently, yet anxiously, at those still rigid features, and a bitter smile of triumph curled his lip, while the hot passionate blood mounted to his hitherto pale cheeks, as his lustful loving gaze dwelt upon that swan-like neck and exquisitely moulded bust.

Sleep on, fair Ellen! Better that thy sleep be that of death, than awake to the terrible reality of thy position! Better, far better, indeed, had it been for thee had thy graceful form have sunk beneath the heaving billows, than that the arms of the brave sailor had borne thee to that rock!

For the serpent hath thee in her coils, and her sting is death.

Thus, for the space of an hour, did the poor girl remain in her lethargic stupor, and her companion sat eagerly watching for the first signs of recovery. They came at last.

A sigh broke from the hitherto silent form, and

her lips breathed the words, "Charles, dear Charles!"

The eyes of the eager watcher glistened, and he bent his head low down, till his face almost touched her cheeks.

Gradually her eyelids unclosed; the death-like pallor of her face gave place to a hectic flush; she stared wildly for a moment, then started from her rude couch with a wild shriek.

For a moment she gazed abstractedly around her; then, placing her hand to her head, staggered, and would have fallen had not the captain caught her in his arms.

With bewildered and half-affrighted looks she gazed upon his features; then, struggling to release herself from the arms which encircled her form, she almost shrieked, "Where am I? Oh, where am I? You are not Charles; no, no, you are not him! This place! Oh, God! I recollect all now; the storm, the ship on the rocks, the wreck, the foaming waters, and Charles! Charles, where are you?"

And, in an agony of horror, she buried her face in her hands, while scalding tears paced each other rapidly down her cheeks.

If that poor girl's beauty had charmed the heart of the young captain when her cheeks where pale, and her form rigid in insensibility, now that the crimson blood had mounted to her temples, and her bosom rose and fell with the violence of her emotions, that passion was enhanced threefold in his breast, and he impulsively strained the weeping girl to his heart, as the hot blood coursed like molten lead through his veins.

But grief so violent must have an end, and the heart-breaking sobs of the poor girl were succeeded by long-drawn sighs.

"Where am I?" she again asked. "What place is this? How came I here?"

"Give not way so," exclaimed the young captain; "you are safe. I discovered you on the rocks, and brought you hither."

As the tones of his voice fell upon her ears, a slight shiver ran through her frame. Not that his tones were harsh or grating; but an instinctive feeling of dread took possession of her soul.

Involuntarily, she endeavoured to free herself from his embrace; but the arms of the young man grasped her far more tightly, while she could feel his hot breath upon her cheek, and his heart throb violently against her bosom.

That undefined feeling of dread for which it is almost impossible to account seized upon her heart; and, as the deep flush of maiden modesty suffused her neck and shoulders, a tremor of horror ran through her frame, and a cold perspiration broke out upon her temples.

She struggled to free herself from the arms that encircled her; but in vain; his grasp, at each fresh endeavour, only became the more tenacious.

Turning her tearful eyes full upon his face, she exclaimed, in imploring accents:

"Why have you brought me to this strange place?"

"Because it was the nearest to that where you were cast ashore."

"Oh! pardon me," she said, "if I do you wrong; but this wild place frightens me. You have not saved me from death to add to my sufferings? Oh! release me; let me depart from hence to some more genial place."

"Where would you go?" he asked.

"I know not," she replied. "Anywhere from here; anywhere to seek for one dearer to me than mine own existence."

The young captain gave a slight start as she said this. The thought flashed upon his mind that the man he had slain upon the rock was perhaps him she would seek; and, in a moment, he replied:

"Your search would be useless; 'tis seldom that the sea gives up its dead."

"Oh, heaven! has he not escaped?" she cried, in agony. "Have the cruel waves torn him from me, and left me to mourn in sorrow and anguish his untimely end?"

"'Tis useless to mourn for that which is irretrievably lost," was the cool reply. "Better be grateful that you yourself are safe, when all besides have perished."

The young girl looked steadfastly at him, and asked:

"Have you never mourned for a loved one?—never grieved when the cruel hand of fate has struck some dear friend from your side?"

There was a pause for a moment, and then he replied—

"Never."

"Then you have never known sorrow," said Ellen, as a sigh rose to her lips, and the tears again started to her eyes.

In a moment his brow became black as midnight.

"Never know sorrow!" he exclaimed, in passionate tones. "It has made me what I am; it has sapped up the well-springs of my heart, and planted in my bosom a hatred to mankind which nothing can eradicate. It has turned the stream of every generous impulse awry, and has grafted in the heart of a generous youth the passion of a fiend!"

Ellen listened with affrighted soul to these words, and again endeavoured to free herself from his grasp.

Scarce knowing what to say, she exclaimed,

"Pray release me; I am stronger now, and need not your kind support."

A sarcastic smile played around the mouth of the youth as she spoke, and pressing her tighter to his breast, he said:

"Doubtless; but I prefer to hold you in these arms; to feel the beating of your heart against my breast; to gaze into those eyes; to press the velvet softness of those cheeks with my own unhallowed lips; to bask in the sunshine of that beauty which nature has given you; to revel in thy charms, and to live in the happiness of thy caresses!"

Ellen trembled as the words smote her ears, and frantically she struggled to release herself from him.

"O! God," she exclaimed, "why am I doomed to these insults? Oh! if you have one spark of mercy in your heart, release me, and let me hence. Oh! why was I saved from the terrible fate that assailed me to be thus outraged? Why did the waves give me up to be thus tortured? Let go your hold; have mercy, as you hope for it hereafter!"

"Ha, ha!" he laughed, coarsely; "mercy is dead in this heart for ever. I have sued for mercy, but it was denied me. As well might you ask this rock to turn to gold as sue this black and seried heart of mine to feel one spark of mercy. That feeling is dead for ever in this breast; it is callous to every feeling of humanity; lost to every impulse of kindness; dead to every hope. I live but for revenge; my hand is at the throat of all; and heaven's curses are upon my soul!"

"Oh! heaven, help me—save me!"

"You plead in vain! I have saved you but for my own desires. This hand would have thrust you back into the boiling surf, but that I had motives more fierce to urge me to save you. This I have done; and now I claim my reward."

ELLEN PROTECTING CHARLES FROM THE ROVER'S VENGEANCE.

"Oh, heavens!" she exclaimed, still struggling to release herself. "If your heart is so callous to my sufferings, will not the memory of a sister, a mother—"

"Hold!" he almost shrieked, whilst his hand grasped her wrist as in a vice. "If there is one word could urge me on to greater crimes, it is that word "mother." I would spare woman the misery I would inflict upon you but for the recollection of a mother's wrongs. Had there been one soft spot in my breast, that word had hardened it to stone: it is the watchword to your ruin, and your own lips have confirmed your doom."

Pale, breathless, and exhausted with her vain struggles to free herself, she gasped forth again—

"Mercy, mercy!"

"Ha, ha!" he laughed, scornfully, whilst the veins upon his forehead stood out prominently, like blue cords upon a polished marble. "You plead in vain; you plead in vain."

And, as he spoke, he forced her towards the rude couch on which she had been reclining.

Again she renewed her frantic struggles to release herself; and, as she seized his hand in her endeavours, she shrieked out—

"Away, away! See, there is blood upon your hands, as well as on your soul!"

"Ha!" he exclaimed, in brutal tones, "it is your lover's."

Wild and piercing was the shriek that echoed

2

through the cavern, as, with almost superhuman strength, she grasped him by the throat.

"Villain! murderer! man or devil! who art thou!"

"Hear and tremble! I am the Boy Rover, the Smuggler of the South Seas, captain of the "Venomed Snake," whose trail is blood, and whose sting is death. Aye, I am he—the terror of the main, the dread of everyone, and the fear of mankind."

"And a coward," was the bold reply, "whose base heart can degrade his brute strength, and debase the man, by outraging a defenceless woman. Shame upon your boasted power! I despise it. In heaven do I place my trust. Back, villain! There is poison in the very air you breathe; contamination in your touch. Back! I say; for I scorn, contemn, and loathe thee."

Stung to madness by her taunts, he seized her roughly in his arms, and bore her to the couch. Vain and frantic were her endeavours to release herself.

Down upon the rude couch he forced her; and it required all his brute strength to accomplish this, so fearfully did she struggle. Her hands were lacerated, and her strength was deserting her; she was fast losing consciousness, and in another minute the villain would triumph. She felt his hot breath upon her cheek, and she shrieked in horror. There was a loud report; a fearful crash; a cry of pain! The ruffian's grip relaxed; and her head sank back as the Boy Rover fell heavily to the ground.

CHAPTER V.

THE CONCEALED LOVER—THE MYSTERY— WOMAN'S FAITH.

When Charles Lawson (for such was the name of the young sailor whom we last saw ensconce himself in one of the casks which formed the supports of the rude table of the cave) found that all attempts were unavailing to raise the heavy weight placed above his head, he almost gave way to despair. He felt that escape from the cave without discovery was now impossible; and bitterly did he regret that he had not trusted to his own courage to meet the men whose voices he had heard in conversation, and stand his chance of escape.

But, after a few moments' calm reflection, he came to the decision that all regrets were useless, and he must now endeavour to devise some means by which he could liberate himself from his confinement.

Certain it is, he thought, that there were other means of entering this cave than by the opening through which he had gained admittance; and, therefore, he felt that if he could release himself from his present uncomfortable situation, he would soon be able to find his way from the cave, and to liberty.

He tried to think calmly, but his mind would wander to the fair girl who had been parted from him by the waves, and the anxiety as to her fate kept his brain in such a whirl of excitement that he could not conjure up to his mind any means by which he could accomplish his purpose.

Thus, bewildered by anxiety for her and liberty for himself, it was with feelings of horror and joy combined that he heard the conversation between the Boy Rover and his followers.

With ears glued, as it were, to the side of that barrel, did he listen to every word that passed, and his heart beat against his breast as though it would force itself from its tenement, as he breathlessly listened for one sound of that fair girl's voice.

But, after the men had left the cave, not a sound broke the stillness, and he would have believed the cave to have been deserted by all but himself, had he not plainly heard the last words of the captain.

Painful, indeed, was that silence to him; for it conjured up to his mind the most dismal forebodings. He could plainly understand the significant words he had heard, and his imagination pictured vividly to his mind the fair and lovely Ellen outraged within his very presence, and himself powerless to aid her.

For, although he had no means of telling that it was the fond idol of his heart who had fallen into the hands of those ruthless wreckers, still that inward voice assured him that it was her, and not all the arguments he could bring forward could convince him to the contrary.

What, then, must have been the misery of those anxious moments as he listened for the first sound of her voice?

And it came at last—came upon his ears in tones of agony—which struck deep into his soul, with the poignancy of a barbed arrow.

His generous heart bounded with joy at the knowledge that she had been saved from a watery grave; but it almost died within him when he recollected to what a fearful fate she was now consigned.

Better that she should lie a corpse at the bottom of the boundless ocean, than live to endure the horrible tortures and meet the degrading fate intended for her by that ruthless band of ruffians, to whom woman's sufferings were sport, and woman's virtue a thing to be violated at pleasure.

Who, then, can imagine the fearful horror of that imprisoned lad as he listened to the interview between the Boy Rover and his lovely captive? Who can describe the fearful agony of his mind when he heard the cruel words of the young smuggler? And who can pourtray the feelings of his breast at the determined struggles of that girl in defence of her honour?

Worked up to a desperation maddening in its intensity, he endeavoured to force the staves of the cask; but too firmly were they bound by their iron girders. Cold drops of perspiration broke out upon his brow, and his brain whirled with the intensity of his sufferings. Then his heart would sink within him, and he would give way to despair; but truly to arouse himself to redoubled energy as he heard the Rover's words, and could judge, by the struggles going on, of the critical moment which had arrived.

Summoning all his strength for a final effort, he forced his knees against the side of the cask, and, pressing his head and hands against the board, strove, with almost superhuman strength, to raise it.

It yielded but an inch; but, through the opening thus made, he saw all that was going on; he saw that fair girl struggling and battling in defence of her honour; he saw that powerful lad, with brutal violence, thrusting her back upon the couch; and he saw the look of mingled misery, horror, and despair upon the features of the woman he so fondly loved.

He thrust the barrel of one of the pistols into the opening between the board and the cask; and, as Ellen shrieked aloud in her agony, he pulled the trigger. He heard the report as it rang, like a clap of thunder, around that stone apartment; he saw the villain's hold on that fair girl's form relax, and, as the Boy Rover fell to the earth, with a burst of gratitude, he exclaimed—

"Thank God, I have saved her!"

And, with this burst of gratitude to heaven, he sank backwards into his small prison, faint and almost powerless from his almost superhuman exertions.

He left the barrel of the pistol firmly wedged between the cask and the board, and thereby left himself an opening through which he could observe all that took place. Besides he thought it would not be politic to give himself the chance of having again to lift the heavy weight which had so fearfully tried his strength.

He did not doubt but that the report of the weapon would be heard by either one or other of the men who were on the watch, and, with a beating heart, he awaited their coming.

He had before dreaded discovery in that cave; but now he felt that his chance of life was of little value; for, had they been inclined to show him mercy, he could not expect that now at their hands, since he had attempted the life of their captain.

It was not long ere Ned and Jim entered, which they did hurriedly.

They had heard the report of the pistol, and imagined that their captain had taken summary vengeance on the poor girl, for some reason or another.

But when they saw the Boy Rover lying prostrate upon the ground, they turned an inquiring look upon each other. Surprise seemed absolutely to deprive them of speech.

Ned was the first to break the silence, which he did by saying—

"Well, I'm blowed!"

"So am I," returned Jim.

And then they looked at each other; then at the captain; then at the girl; and then at each other again.

It was evident that there was a mystery, which neither could solve; and so they gazed from those prostrate forms into each other's face, till they both exclaimed again, simultaneously—

"Well, I'm blowed!"

There was another pause a few moments' duration; and then Ned, stooping down, raised the head of the Boy Rover on his knee, and peered into his face.

There was a thin streak of blood on his left cheek; and his face was otherwise deathly pale.

"Shot, by Davey!" he exclaimed.

"Then that gal's done it," said Jim; and yet she don't seem to have come too yet. But where's the pistol?"

"Don't know," was the answer.

"Then why don't you look for it? It couldn't have been done with a pop-gun."

"Well, I don't suppose it was. But here— just pour some of this down his throat, and see if that won't wake him up."

Jim took the flask, which still contained some brandy, from the table, and gave it to Ned, who immediately commenced to pour some of the spirit down the throat of the insensible boy.

"There's one thing to say," said Ned, "if it don't bring him up again, it won't do him much harm. But I'm blowed if I think that ere gal did it; I don't believe she's got strength enough in her to pull a trigger."

"It's a rum go, that's all I knows; and I don't think he's such a fool as to shoot himself."

"Don't know," replied Ned; "he's such a rum chap at times."

"Well, he is," said the other, looking about in the hopes of discovering the weapon; "but, if that gal did it, she's swallowed the pistol, so as there should be no evidence against her—that's all I got to say."

And so saying, he approached the couch, and thrust his hand down by the side of Ellen to feel for the weapons.

Slowly the Boy Rover's eyelids opened, and he gazed in bewilderment from the face of one to the face of the other.

"How are you now, captain?" asked Ned. "Here, take another pull at this; it will revive you."

And again he placed the flask to his mouth.

"Take it away!" exclaimed the Boy Rover, as with one bound he leapt to his feet.

"What's been the matter, captain?" asked Jim.

The youth gazed from one to the other, with a half-surprised, half-doubting look; then placing his hand to his head, and withdrawing it, he perceived it was covered with blood.

"Well, captain," remarked Ned, "I rather think you've had a narrow squeak; but it ain't done for you, that's certain."

"How did it happen, captain?" asked Jim.

Still the Boy Rover gazed intently into their eyes, with a look of doubt upon his face.

"Look you," he said, at length, "if either of you want to get rid of me, say so, and strike before my face."

It was Ned and Jim who now looked doubtfully at the captain.

"You ain't quite right yet," said Ned. "Here, take another pull; it'll do you good."

And again he proffered the flask.

But the Boy Rover struck it fiercely from his hand.

"What!" he exclaimed, savagely—"finding that the bullet has failed in its mission, you would now finish your work by poison? Speak —is it so?"

If Ned and Jim were surprised before, they were doubly so now; and, after exchanging glances with each other, and ominously shaking their heads, Ned exclaimed—

"Quite off his chump—quite!"

To this opinion Jim nodded his thorough conviction.

"Which of you," demanded the captain, "fired that shot?"

"Which of us?" echoed Ned.

"Yes."

"Why, neither," said Jim.

"Who did it, then?"

"That's just what we want to know," said Jim. "It wasn't the gal—was it?"

"The girl!" said the captain. "No."

"Then it must have been yourself," said Jim, "a trying to commit fellow-de-see."

The eyes of the boy captain were fixed piercingly upon the features of his two followers: he was trying to read there the mystery of that shot which had so nearly deprived him of life, and sent him to account for those sins for which he would surely have to answer.

But he could trace nothing in the looks and manners of these men, and he seated himself on the edge of the couch, surprised and puzzled in the extreme.

"Which of you," he said, after a pause, "was on watch at the mouth of the cave?"

"I was," said Ned.

"Who passed you?"

"Nobody."

"Did you desert your post for a moment? Speak the truth; and if you did, I'll forgive you."

"I wish I may die, captain, if I did!" exclaimed the man in the most emphatic tones.

"It is strange," said the Boy Rover, musingly. "That I have been shot, there is the proof," he added, as he placed his hand to his face, and withdrew it covered with blood.

"There ain't no mistake about that," remarked Jim, "because we heard the report; and that's how we came to leave our posts."

"Have you searched the cave?"

"Well, we can see there's nobody here but ourselves and the gal; and if she didn't do it, and you didn't do it, then I'm blowed if it mustn't have been a ghost!" said Ned.

"Fool!" exclaimed the Boy Rover, "that pistol was fired by human hands. Some one must have gained admittance. But how—how?"

"I know a mouse couldn't have passed me," said Ned, "without my seeing it; so, if anybody got in here, they must have come by some other way than the passage."

"There is but one other," said the captain—"the opening to the sea—and that I closed myself. There is a mystery in this I am determined to fathom; and when I have fathomed it, woe to him that fired that shot!"

Ellen now gave signs of recovery; and, perceiving this, the Boy Rover ordered the two men once more to their posts.

He was at a loss to understand the events of the last half hour, but he felt convinced in his own mind that both Ned and Jim were innocent of the attempt upon his life.

Could that girl, unseen by him, have perpetrated the deed? That could not be; for was she not firmly pinioned by his arms?

He could not fathom it, and he therefore gave it up for the present, at all events, and turned to the now recovering girl.

The wound was not a dangerous one; the bullet had glanced along his cheek, and grazed the side of his temple; but it had stunned him for the time, as we have seen, and the only evil effect was a violent headache. Had the position of his head been once further, either way, the career of the Boy Rover would have been ended.

With returning consciousness came returning misery; and no sooner did the glance of poor Ellen rest upon the form of the Boy Rover than with one bound she sprang from the couch, and stood in the centre of the cave.

She feared that he would again endeavour to effect his purpose; and once more she summoned both her wits and her strength to her aid.

She resolved to meet death rather than dishonour, and she prepared herself for any emergency that might happen.

And thus she stood, like a beautiful tiger at bay, awaiting the first movement of the hunter.

Oh! had she but known that her lover was concealed beneath that rude table, and that two shining barrels were ready to belch forth their deadly fire (for he had placed the still charged pistol in that small crevice, reloaded the one which he had fired, and returned it to its former position), how her heart would have leaped for joy, and, instead of awaiting the assault, would have almost felt inclined to become the assailant.

With a woman's spirit, she would have avenged a woman's wrongs.

But the boy captain had no further intention of molesting her that night. He had resolved that she should fall a victim to his unholy passions; but for the present she was safe.

His first assault had ended in defeat; but in the second he resolved to win the victory.

"You need have no fear of me," he exclaimed —"for the present you are safe. To-night you may rest in peace; but I have resolved you shall yet fall. Your fiery spirit, and bold resistance, has strengthened the resolve. Think to-night how vain is that resistance, and prepare to-morrow to meet your doom."

"Villain!—there is a God above us, who never turns a deaf ear to the oppressed. He will shield the weak against the strong, and protect the defenceless in the hour of need."

"Ha, ha, ha!" laughed the boy captain, scornfully. "Put your trust in heaven; but, spite of all, you shall fall."

"Scoffer!" she exclaimed, "already has it sent me aid, and when needed will do so again."

The Boy Rover started at these words. He was not superstitious, but the mystery of the bullet which grazed his cheek, and the words of the young girl, uttered in that firm self-convinced tone, set the mind of that blood-stained youth wondering whether heaven did send aid to the virtuous and oppressed.

Sure it is that Providence, in its own good time, punishes the guilty. Vice may triumph for awhile; but, in the end, innocence and virtue will rise upon its downfall.

Finding that Ellen did not attempt to move, and still watched his every movement with suspicion, he said—

"I have promised not to molest you again to-night, and I will keep my word. This rude cave is ill-suited to your company; but to-morrow's sun shall see you better provided for. In the cabin of the 'Venomed Snake' you will meet with every luxury that you can hope for. There you will find your every wish supplied—your every command obeyed. There you shall remain mistress of all; and the only return I ask is your love."

Helen listened patiently till he had done; and then her tall handsome form was drawn up to its full height, and, with flashing eyes and scornfully curled lip, she replied—

"I have listened to your insults, and if I have not interrupted your speech, it was because contempt held me powerless to speak? Is it possible that one can be so lost to all respect for the feelings of a poor unhappy girl as to insult her misery, and enhance her sufferings, by the offer of such an honour? Do you think that the comforts and luxuries, as you term them, of a rover's cabin, can compensate me for the loss of friends and honour? No, though you were to lay the wealth of the world at my feet, still would I scorn you! Here I stand, a poor weak and defenceless girl, without a friend to aid me in my suffering; but with my trust in Him who helps the widow and the fatherless, I will resist to the last your infamous designs—while one spark of life remains in this weak frame I will battle in defence of that jewel dearer to woman than her very existence. Rather would I dash my brains out at your feet than that you should triumph over my virtue.

I hold my honour dearer than life; therefore will I freely, freely sacrifice my life in its defence."

Proud and defiant was the demeanour of that fair girl as she gave utterance to those words; and the tones of her voice carried to the ears of the Boy Rover the conviction of her determination to resist him to the last.

Little did he dream of the heroic courage to be found in woman when driven to despair; little did he know how fixed and unflinching is woman's resolve!

He had imagined that, perhaps, the prospect of meeting with every luxury on board his bark, would have tempted her to look more favourably upon him. But he was undeceived. He could now see that her abhorrence of him was equally as great as before he spoke of his vessel and its comforts; and, with ill-suppressed rage, he returned.

"I will humble your proud spirit yet. I have marked you out for my own, and you shall yet submit. You have braved me, but as yet you know not my power. You shall fall—ay, fall at my feet in shame—and that virtue you so much prize shall remain but a memory of the past."

"Liar!" she almost shrieked.

"And no power on earth shall save you," he exclaimed, as his face reddened with passion. "You have scorned me, but you shall yet find that the Boy Rover will triumph—ay, triumph."

And, casting a look upon her full of hate, he turned and rapidly left the cavern, leaving Ellen standing in its centre, her bosom heaving violently, with feelings of scorn and indignation.

And thus she stood, till the last echoes of his footsteps died away; then, approaching the couch, she sank down on her knees beside it, and, burying her face in her hands, burst into tears.

CHAPTER VI.

WITH feelings better to be imagined than described Charles Lawson had heard and seen all that had passed; and often, indeed, did his fingers stray to the trigger of one or the other of the pistols, and as often did he withdraw his hand as he thought that the second shot might prove more fatal to himself than the first had done.

True it was that he might succeed in depriving the world of the presence of a ruffian who was a disgrace to humanity; but then, should he be discovered and slain, who would protect that poor girl?

Better, he thought, deprive himself of the pleasure of shooting the villain so long as he attempted no further violence to Ellen, and trust to something to turn up to release him from his present confinement and giving him a chance of effecting the escape of both.

It was with a feeling of joy, therefore, that he saw the Boy Rover stride from the cave.

He listened intently for a few moments and then finding that he did not return, he placed his hands to his mouth so as to guide his voice towards the couch and called out in a loud whisper.

"Ellen!"

But the poor girl was so overwhelmed with grief that she did not hear him.

Again he repeated her name, but still she heard him not.

Once more he essayed to speak, and this time in a louder tone.

"Ellen—dear Ellen!"

The young girl raised her head and looked around in bewildered amazement, then heaving a heavy sigh, once more buried her face in her hands.

In an agony of feeling, he once more called out:

"Ellen, Ellen, fear not! It is me, Charles."

With a suppressed scream she started up, and gazed, half-frightened, around the cave.

"That voice!" she gasped. "Merciful heavens—there is no one there; and yet I thought I heard his voice."

"Ellen, Ellen," was again repeated.

She clasped her forehead, and staggered towards the rude table, as she muttered:

"Oh God! is this madness that is seizing upon me? Have the sufferings that I have endured turned my brain?"

"No, dear Ellen, you are not mad," exclaimed the young man. "'Tis me—Charles—myself. Fear not; I am near you; but I cannot come to your side—I am imprisoned."

"Where—where?" she almost shrieked.

"Hush, hush!" was the reply. "Here, beneath this rude table. Speak low; here, here!"

With a cry of joy she stooped and looked beneath the board.

"Where?" she again asked; but this time in a low tone of voice.

"In this cask, dear Ellen, powerless to move from the weight above me."

"Oh! heaven, I thank thee," she murmured; "for thou hast not deserted me in the hour of misery."

"Ellen," said the young man, "look around the cave, and see if you can find anything which you can insert between the board and this cask, and thus assist me to move the great weight. Be silent; let not a sound reach the ears of those cruel wretches, or we are lost."

Oh! with what anxiety did she look for something to assist in moving that board. For some moments she was unsuccessful; but at the farther end of the cove was a piece of plank, about four feet in length. This she seized eagerly, and returned to the table.

The eyes of the imprisoned youth watched her every movement, with the utmost anxiety.

"Stoop down," he said.

She did so.

"Look," he added, "the board is raised about an inch from the top of the cask. Place the end of that plank in the crevice; then bear all your strength upon the other end."

She forced one end of the plank into the crevice, and leant her whole weight on the other end, as Charles had bidden her; whilst he, at the same time, exerted all his strength to assist in raising the board.

Their united exertions were successful, and that board moved slowly along the top of the cask till it left about one-third of its circumference bare.

With a cry of joy she bent over it; and in a moment the arms of the young man were encircled around her neck.

"Ellen," he exclaimed, "dear, dear Ellen, I have heard all that passed between you and that heartless wretch; and the agony that I endured almost drove me to distraction. But fear not; I will protect you against his villainous designs; whilst one drop of blood remains in this frame, it shall be sacrificed for you. Here Ellen," he added, as he held up the pistols, "take these weapons while I extricate my cramped body from this cask. Be careful; they are lended; already one of them has struck your friend, and shall again, Ellen, if necessity requires."

"Ah!" returned the now delighted girl, "I see now how timely aid came to my rescue when power and strength were leaving me. Oh! Charles, how can this poor heart feel sufficiently grateful for this preservation; and how can my tongue find words to express that gratitude?"

"It was the will of Providence," returned the youth, "and to that providence our prayers are due."

As he spoke he squeezed his body out of the cask, but it was with considerable difficulty that he did so, for his limbs had become stiff and cramped in his small hiding-place, and his wet garments added in no small degree to impede his progress.

But he thought not of his own uncomfortable position, it was that fair girl's safety only that he cared for, and her release from that place where she had been submitted to such cruelty.

"Ellen," he exclaimed, as he once more threw his arms around the form of the maiden! "your sufferings have indeed been fearful. It was cruel destiny to be wrecked so near at home, but it was worse to fall into the hands of these monsters. But we must escape them, dear one: never shall you be again subjected to the agony you have but now endured. Those pistols will perhaps save us. I will shoot these wretches and gain our freedom."

"Charles,".returned Ellen, trembling with emotion, "vengeance is not for us; they would slay you, but shall we take that life which it is not in our power to return. No, leave them to the laws of their country and their God!"

"Noble-minded girl," he exclaimed, as he imprinted an impassioned kiss upon her lips; "your generous heart would extend mercy to those who have so deeply wronged you; but he has forfeited all right to it. Ruthlessly would he have sacrificed you to his unholy lust; unfeelingly would he have trampled upon your peace of mind—savagely would he have destroyed your happiness for ever! Mercy for him—mercy for the wanton wretch who cannot grant it even to a woman—mercy for the base reptile who has not one spark of feeling in his soul? No! he has violated every principle of honour and feeling—he has set alike the laws of God and man at defiance—he has forfeited every right to mercy, and he shall die!"

And the brave youth took one of the pistols in his hand, and, with clenched teeth and darkened brow, strode towards the passage.

Trembling with fear for his safety, she seized his arm, and, gazing tenderly in his face, while the tears filled her lustrous eyes, she said—

"Charles, if I can forgive the wrongs he has done me, can you wish to stain your soul with the blood of him who is as base as you are noble? Oh! let us endeavour to escape from hence without bloodshed; let us not have upon our conscience the crime of murder."

The soft sweet tones of her voice, the appealing look she fixed upon him, and the gentle, yet firm, pressure of the hand upon his arm, to stay his progress, caused him to pause, and fixing on her a look full of love and tenderness, he replied:

"Ellen, you are an angel, and your woman's heart does honour to your sex. Let him live, then, to answer to those laws he has outraged. For your sake this hand of mine shall not be raised against his life, unless by any act of his own he rush upon his destruction."

"Knows he aught of your being here?" asked Ellen, suddenly.

"No," replied the youth; "I entered this cave during the absence of himself and his hellish band —not by the way you were brought here, but from the sea."

"His band?" said Ellen, in a tone of surprise.

"Yes, dear one: from what I overheard, he is evidently the captain of as desperate a set of ruffians as ever lived. He is a wrecker and a smuggler; and the light which we saw shining so brightly over the waves was in this cave—a false beacon, which was contrived to lure us to destruction."

"And well indeed has it played its part. Perhaps you and I are the only survivors of this cruel night's work."

"Indeed, I fear it is so," replied the youth, with a sigh. "Few, indeed, would survive amid those fearful breakers. I succeeded in grasping a portion of the wreck, and was carried on to this rock; and, by the aid of a rope, succeeded in landing myself in this cavern. But how did you succeed in reaching the shore?"

"I don't know," replied Ellen. "I felt myself being drawn under the waves, and sense was fast leaving me, when some one grasped me in their arms. I recollect no more till I recovered from my swoon, and found myself in this place."

"And to the villanous treatment you have received at the hands of that lawless youth?"

"Yes. But is there more than one outlet to this place? I can see none but the one yonder, through which my persecutor has gone."

"That is the one by which you were brought here. There is another, which is evidently used for the landing of their spoil. 'Tis here, and looks out upon the sea."

The youth walked to the spot where the fire had been burning, and examined the covering to the opening. Then pushing the rude doorway aside, disclosed to the gaze of Ellen the open sea beneath them.

The fair girl laid her hand upon his shoulder, and, pointing out, exclaimed—

"Charles, there lies the road to liberty, should all other means fail."

The young man gazed at her, as though he could not understand her meaning.

"How?" he asked.

"Should all other means fail, we will leap from the place into the waves, and trust to Heaven to guide us to safety."

"But we should be dashed to pieces ere we reached the water," he answered. "It would be madness; nay, almost certain death."

"Better meet that, Charles, than dishonour. Better, far better, that we should meet in heaven in purity and peace, than that I should live a thing broken in spirit, and loathsome to myself."

"Ellen," exclaimed the youth, while his tones trembled with emotion, "I care not for myself. If I can but succeed in releasing you from the power of these wretches—if I could but feel that you were in safety—I would submit to all the misery they could inflict upon me; for willingly would I sacrifice my love to preserve yours."

"Well, dear Charles, she answered, "do I know your generous nature; but you must not endanger yourself for me alone. If I die, for never till death has claimed me will I yield to the unholy passions of this daring smuggler, I shall leave but few to mourn me and suffer by my loss. But you, Charles, have much to live for. Life is but just opening upon you; 'tis now but the dawn of a future, bright and prosperous, upon which that existence must set. You have a mother, whose gray hairs would be bowed with sorrow to the grave should aught ill befall you. I have no right to expect you to sacrifice yourself for my sake. You may singly make your escape from the place; but trammelled by me, you may perish, and I should have the sad reflection, to enhance my misery, that I had been instrumental in your destruction.

A look of pain and sorrow crossed the features of the brave lad as Ellen gave utterance to these words; and, in a voice half choked by the violence of his feelings, he exclaimed, in a wounded tone:

"Oh! Ellen, do you no longer love me?"

"Love you, Charles?" she exclaimed, as she pressed his hand between her soft fingers. "It is that undying love for you that prompts me to urge you to seek your own safety; that love which cannot, will not, be selfish enough to lead you into further danger. Should you fall, nothing but the memory of that love would remain, like a bright star shining from a dark cloud—an oasis in the arid desert—but one happy thought to dwell upon when all is misery, despair, and wretchedness."

The head of the poor girl sank upon the bosom of the youth, as he fondly pressed her to his heart. A proud look overspread his features, and drawing himself up to his full height, in a tone of pride, he exclaimed:

"By that love do I stand or fall! Look," he added, drawing her towards the opening, and pointing out upon the sea—" on those dancing billows, I have met dangers in many forms; but never once have feared to meet my fate, whatever it may have been. I have stood upon the deck of my gallant bark when the storm has raged in furious wrath, and has every instant threatened us with destruction. The heavens have belched forth their fires upon the bark, and struck my comrades down by my side. Still have I not quailed; for I have put my trust in Him who commands the winds and the waves. Ellen, within this breast, beats the heart of a British seaman, and may Heaven desert me if ever I degrade my profession, and disgrace the proud flag under which I have sailed, by refusing to succour a woman in distress or shielding to the last drop of blood, the girl I love!"

The heart of Ellen swelled within her bosom as she listened to these words, and she encircled her smooth, white, rounded, arms about his neck, and imprinted a kiss of passionate fervour upon his brow.

If she had loved that brave youth before, how much more ardently did she love him now! The words he uttered had sent the warm blood coursing through her veins, and suffusing her face with a blush of pride. They seemed to imbue her limbs with a firmness and strength hitherto unknown, and to engraft in her bosom a feeling of courage to meet any danger by his side that might present itself.

"Generous Charles, my heart must indeed be cold," she murmured, "did it not bound with joy at your words. Proudly you claim it, and nobly you would defend it. By our loves we will stand or fall, live or die. Come weal or woe, we will live and die together!"

"Bravely spoken, Ellen!" he exclaimed. "With the knowledge that we battle in a righteous cause and with a firm trust in Heaven's aid, we shall yet triumph over our enemies, and escape from this accursed place."

"Or perish in the attempt!" exclaimed a voice close behind them.

The lovers started round as these words fell upon their ears; and Ellen with difficulty suppressed the scream of fear which rose to her lips.

The Boy Rover, and his two followers, stood glaring upon them. The young smuggler had a short cutlass in his hand, which he held menacingly towards Charles.

But the brave boy quailed not at the sight of these reckless young men; but, casting a hurried look around the cave, darted towards the rude table, to repossess himself of the pistols, which he placed there when he drew the partition from the opening to the sea.

But as he stretched forth his hand to reach them his foot caught in a coil of rope which lay on the floor of the cave, and he fell heavily to the ground.

With a cry of horror Ellen clasped her hands in despair. The Boy Rover sprang forward and placed his foot upon the body of the prostrate youth.

"Fool," he hissed, "you, then, it was who attempted my life, and now would rob me of my mistress. Fool! you have rushed upon your doom."

He raised the cutlass above his head to strike, but ere it could descend Ellen stood before him with a pistol in each hand presented at his head.

She had bounded forward and obtained possession of the weapons, and now stood ready to protect his life, or avenge his death.

The Boy Rover recoiled a few paces as that brave girl stood over the prostrate body of her lover.

"Advance one step," she exclaimed, in a determined tone—"lower that weapon but an inch to do him harm, and a woman's hand shall protect a brave boy's life, and avenge her outraged honour!"

The Boy Rover, whose daring spirit had never quailed before the greatest danger, now stood irresolute. He saw the proud form of that beautiful girl standing majestically before him, with her fingers pressed upon the triggers and the shining barrels pointing at his head, and for the time he was cowed.

But his was not a nature to give way, for any length of time, to fear; and in a few moments he had revolved in his mind a stratagem by which to disarm her.

Calling out to his followers, he exclaimed—

"Touch the spring; she is standing on the trap, and she will fall through and be dashed to pieces!"

At these words Ellen, with a start, lowered her gaze from the Rover's face and looked down upon the ground. The moment was fatal to her; with one bound the young smuggler threw his arms around her and pinioned her so firmly that she was powerless to move her hands.

"Secure the boy," he roared. "Ha, ha, ha! my pretty one, you see the Boy Rover is one too many for you this time."

Ned and Jim rushed upon the brave youth, as he was rising to his feet, and held him in their strong arms.

In vain were his struggles to free himself from their grasp. The exertions he had undergone had so weakened him, that he seemed, as it were, but a child in the hands of those rough strong men; and, in a few moments, he was bound by a strong cord.

With a countenance overspread with an agonising expression, poor Ellen watched the operation; and, when it was completed, and she saw her brave young lover and protector rendered powerless to help her, she burst into tears, and became almost insensible,

---

CHAPTER VII.

THE BOY ROVER AND HIS CAPTIVES.

"There's many a slip 'twixt the cup and the lip," is an old proverb; and in this instance, perhaps, it was as truly proved as it was possible it could have been.

But a few moments before, both Ellen and her lover had almost felt assured of obtaining their release from the power of the Boy Rover; hope had dawned in their breasts; but, alas! to be dashed aside, to give place to despair.

It was but the bright sunshine for an instant through the dark cloud, to be overspread by one denser and blacker than before.

They both felt that their position was now more desperate than it had hitherto been; and they feared more for the safety of each other than they did for themselves.

In her agony, poor Ellen saw in imagination the form of her lover sacrificed to the brutal passions of those ruthless men; whilst Charles Lawson trembled for the fate of the poor girl, and bitterly cursed his own helplessness.

The Boy Rover guessed the thoughts that were preying upon the minds of both his prisoners, and, with a demoniac smile, he watched the countenances of his victims, and gloated in their misery.

He was the first to speak, and, in measured and determined tones, he said—

"I have been a listener to all that has passed between you, and have discovered the mystery of the shot aimed at my life; and, likewise, the means by which you gained access to this secret cave. You will find your escape from my power somewhat doubtful, as well as difficult. You have attempted my life, and, as mine is a revengeful nature, you can rest assured that I shall not forgive the deed—though doubtless you, and society in general, would have considered it one of the most justifiable. Had you even not attempted my destruction, still I shou'd look upon you as a dangerous enemy; for you know our retreat, and would bring down upon us the officers of justice. So that you perceive that your freedom is that which we least desire, and your death most necessary to our existence. I have spoken thus much, so that you may entertain no hope of mercy at our hands."

There was a proud look in the eye of the young sailor as the Boy Rover waited to hear his reply.

He had not to wait long, for, in a firm tone, he said—

"Cowardly ruffian! I have heard you to the end because I am powerless to stay you. I scorn to sue for mercy to one so base and degraded as yourself. For myself I care nothing; but if their be one spark of humanity in your bosom—if every sense of feeling is not obliterated in that callous heart—have mercy on the fair being you hold in your arms. Stain not your soul with a crime so black that humanity must shudder in horror at the bare thought of. Have mercy on her! I am a British seaman, and have sailed under the colours that never struck to slave or dastard; and I scorn to bemean myself by asking quarter at your hands. But, I beg, plead, pray of you to have mercy on her! Villain your actions prove you to be; but if one drop of

English blood runs in your veins, taint it not by the base and degrading name of coward: for a mean and despicable coward must he indeed be who can outrage a defenceless woman. 'Tis the act of a brute, who possesses not one spark of humanity; 'tis the crime of the cur, who forfeits all right to mercy at the hands of his fellow-men; a deed which would render you the despised of man, the accursed of heaven, and the abhorred of hell!"

Jim and Ned having seen that Charles was now powerless to do any harm walked to the end of the passage, and the Boy Rover having possessed himself of the pistols which Ellen had threatened his life with a few moments before, led her to the rude couch, and then advancing to the opening through which herself and lover had gazed forth upon the sea; he closed the partition, and once more confronted the bound youth.

"Fine sentiments," he exclaimed, sarcastically; "your friends have mistaken your forte—they should have made you a parson instead of a sailor; in that line you would have made a fortune, and doubtless have earned a destination which few in your hazardous calling obtain. On my ears your words fall needlessly. I have taken a fancy to this girl and resistance to my wishes but adds fuel to my passions. I look upon her as my lawful prize; I have saved her from destruction——"

"But to inflict upon her a misery worse than a thousand deaths," interrupted the young sailor. "Ah, coward—coward!"

"As you will, my brave fellow," exclaimed the Rover, as he bit his lip with vexation at the emphasis Charles laid upon the word; "as you will, but nevertheless I tell you she shall succumb."

"Never, liar!" exclaimed the youth, "she is too pure, too good. Rather will she meet death a thousand times than yield to such a wretch as you!"

The Boy Rover clenched his fist, and bit his lips to suppress his rising passion.

"There is a limit, he exclaimed, "to every one's forbearance, so beware!"

Proudly the young sailor drew himself up, and casting a scornful, withering glance upon the Rover, he exclaimed—

"I fear not your menaces. I repeat it—coward and liar!"

With the yell of a tiger the Boy Rover drew back his arm, and was about to launch a heavy blow at the face of the young sailor, when Ellen started forward and stood between them.

"Coward!" she exclaimed—"aye, despicable coward!—would you strike one who is powerless to protect himself? Shame on you—shame! Strike if you will, but with my body do I shield him: strike, and let thy dastard hand fall upon a woman's breast!"

The Boy Rover's arm drooped to his side, and villain that he was, he stood abashed before the scornful look of that young fair girl, as, throwing her arms around her lover's neck, she shielded him with her body.

"Let him do his worst," said Charles, with a look of tenderness at his fair preserver. "Still do I scorn him with his threats. With my arms free, surely would he fly like a raven cur from my presence."

"Oh, waste not words upon him," said Ellen, as her bosom rose and fell with the violence of her emotion; "he is alike worthless and contemptible. His base nature triumphs now in our

CHARLES AND ELLEN ESCAPING FROM THE CAVERN.

misery, but a day of retribution will come when he will not go scatheless. Heed him not, Providence will yet send us aid to thwart his hellish designs."

"Dear Ellen," murmured the youth, "I could bear all the misery, all the insults he could inflict upon me; but you, you——"

"Fear not for me," interrupted the young girl. "I am strong in my resolve never to submit to him. He may kill me, but never dishonour me. No, no! —welcome death!—but never shall you blush for the girl who has bestowed on you her love."

"I know it, Ellen; I feel it."

"Heed him not, then, and let him do his worst."

The Boy Rover listened to the conversation with

feelings of rage and mortification. He clenched his hands, and bit his lips with passion; but the calm scornful glance of the young girl's eye cowed his brutal nature, and he feared to strike.

He grasped the arm of the young girl in his iron grip, and he hissed between his teeth as he scowled revengefully upon her—

"You defy and scorn me; but you shall feel my power. You have called me liar and coward; and you shall find that I am one, but not the other. I will break the haughty spirits of yourself and him you call your love. I will make you that which is loathsome to yourself; and he shall be the instrument I will use for your destruction. Nay, frown if you will, I heed not your scornful looks. I will bring the blush of shame to your cheeks, plant the canker-worm of misery in your heart, and make your life a very hell of horror and despair."

"Fiend! devil! I despise your threats, and laugh to scorn your boasting lies."

And, with an indignant and scornful laugh, she flung his rude grasp from her own.

Foaming with rage, the Boy Rover strode towards the passage where his companions stood; then, turning, he exclaimed—

"Remember my words. You have defied me: you have scorned the Boy Rover—the dreaded smuggler of the South Seas—one who never forgets or forgives. Though I wade through rivers of blood to encompass your ruin, you shall yet be mine. The 'Venomed Snake' is making every preparation to sail; once on board, you shall both feel the power I possess. There shall be no torture too fearful for your lover that I will not invent; and his sufferings shall be the stepping-stones to my success. So beware of him whose love you have scorned—of the Boy Rover, who is now your bitterest foe."

And, motioning to Ned and Jim to follow him, he hastily darted down the passage, and was lost to sight.

CHAPTER VIII.

THE BOY ROVER AND HIS COMPANIONS IN CRIME—THE SUSPICION.

CHAFING with rage, the Boy Rover strode on, followed by his two companions, Ned and Jim, till he had reached the open air. His savage nature had been partly cowed by the calm determination and bearing of the young lovers; and, like the brute who is only tamed by the steady gaze of the unflinching eye, he feared to make the spring, and for the time his brutal nature became dormant.

But his determination to possess the young girl was not for one moment shaken; resistance but added fuel to the flames that were consuming him, and he now set himself to think of some diabolical means by which he could drag down the young and virtuous maiden to his wishes.

He saw plainly that she dearly loved the youth who had so mysteriously found his way into the secret cave; and he felt that in him lie the instrument of his success. He could see that no torture, however hellish, inflicted upon herself, would cause her to become a willing victim; but he thought, "to save him she loves, she may sacrifice herself." He resolved, then, to bear them both on board the "Venomed Snake," and let her witness the indignities and cruelties he would inflict upon her lover, and make her consent the only means by which she could save his life.

As these thoughts passed through his brain, a sardonic smile played around his mouth, and he felt sure in his own mind that he would yet conquer.

Gradually the fury of his passions wore themselves out, and he almost laughed outright at the imagination of his success.

Alas! for the immutability of human hopes—success is not always certain. 'Tis a phantom, that often vanishes at the touch. We stretch forth our hand to grasp the substance, but find, to our chagrin and disappointment, we clutch but at a shadow.

But to the young mind the certainty of ultimate success most always presents itself, whether it be for good or evil. Nor is it till disappointment falls upon them with its overwhelming crushing weight,

that they realise the truth that the substance is sometimes lost by grasping at the shadow.

The Boy Rover felt that the substance was indeed in his grasp; and firm was the hold he meant to keep upon it, to prevent its eluding his clutch.

With that youth firmly bound, and powerless to aid her, he thought now how easy would be his triumph over the poor girl, and how exquisitely demoniac should be the means employed to that youth whom she so fondly loved, to assure that consummation.

The man that grasps at a sunbeam to save himself from falling, strikes his head against the substance he is endeavouring to escape; and then it is he discovers how futile have been his exertions, how vain and absurd his endeavours.

Whether it be for weal or woe, certainty of success is not always realised. We dwell on it till we could sacrifice our life upon the cast; but yet it will disappoint us.

The greater our certainty, the greater our disappointment; and the more we cherish the hope, the more crushing is the failure.

Certainty only—positive certainty of success—reigned in the breast of the Boy Rover, and, with feelings of triumph swelling his unmanly breast, he paced thoughtfully up and down before the entrance to the passage of the cave.

The storm had ceased, and the bright chaste lamp of night sailed proudly in a sea of ethereal blue, high up above his head, and cast its mellow rays of refulgent splendour over the dancing waves, lining their crested tops with a sparkling lustre, and shedding a halo of glory aslant the grave of the brave crew of the doomed bark.

The raging elements had given place to a calm so peaceful and serene, that only the hum of the sea, and the monotonous plash of the waves upon the rocks, broke the now most painful silence. The warring elements had expended their mad fury, and calm serenity now reigned around.

But still the black passions in that young Rover's heart were as deadly as before. The calm of nature found no repose in his blackened soul.

Suddenly he stopped before his companions, and, addressing them, said—

"The moon will go down in an hour: we must then get these prisoners on board, and at once set sail."

"Do you mean taking the lad?" asked Ned, in a tone of surprise.

"I do," answered the captain.

"Why, you don't think he'll join us—do you?" asked Jim, inquiringly.

"He is necessary to the furtherance of my views," said the youth.

"Better drop him over the rocks," remarked Ned; "he'll only be in the way aboard. Besides, captain, I should say you owed him something for that shot."

"And doubt not I will pay him," returned the Boy Rover, as he ground his teeth at the thought of the defiance of the young man.

"Then," said Jim, "I shouldn't have any unnecessary trouble with him. He's bound tight enough now, and won't be able to take a stroke to save himself. Drop him over, I say, and there'll be an end of all trouble about him. Besides, while the girl knows he's all right and safe, she'll never give in."

"And there'll be an end of all fear of his betraying the secret entrance from the sea," remarked Ned.

The Boy Rover became thoughtful.

"No," he said, after a pause, "not yet. For the present he must live; but with the fear of death ever hovering over his head. He must live to be the instrument of bringing that girl to reason."

"Well," said Ned, shrugging his shoulders, "I suppose you know best; but I'm blowed if I think it will answer."

"I will try," said the captain, as he turned away, and continued pacing thoughtfully up and down.

"He's got his match in that gal," said Jim to his companion, in a low tone, as the Boy Rover walked from them; "and it wouldn't surprise me if she don't beat him yet."

"Then she'll be the first as has," exclaimed the other.

"That may be," said Jim; "but then you see she's got more pluck in her than most of her sort; and I'm blessed if I won't bet you my grog for a week that he don't succeed in doing as he likes with that ere gal."

"Hush!" remarked Ned—"if he hears you he may think we intend to prevent him. He's as suspicious as he's daring, and as passionate as the devil. Speak lower."

"Is it a bet?" asked the other, in a low tone.

"No," replied Ned, after a pause; "for I'm blowed if I don't think so too."

"And it strikes me she will," continued Jim; "she's a plucky gal, and if it wasn't that she'd blow the gaff, damme if I shouldn't like to see her get scot free."

"Hush!" said Ned, grasping his companion's arm in a vice-like grip. "Are you mad? If the captain had heard that, there would have been no escape for you."

Jim looked hard in his companion's face, as he replied, in a whisper—

"The words slipped out before I thought."

"Be careful, then, if you value your life," said Ned.

"Well, only you heard them. Would you split?"

And the rough sailor's hand fastened on the knife he carried in his belt.

"No," said Ned, "we have been pals too long to betray each other. But your tongue will endanger your head if you don't keep your thoughts to yourself. We must abide by our oath; and if he wants that gal we must do our best to help him to his wishes."

"Well, that's true; so let our thoughts go no further. We must stick to him through thick and thin, and where he leads we must follow, even though the gallows is our destination."

This conversation was interrupted by the Boy Rover, who once more approached his followers.

"Let us return to the cavern," he said, hurriedly. "We have been mad fools; we have secured the boy, but left the girl the free liberty of her hands."

"Blowed if we ain't, captain," said Ned. "Well, I never thought of that."

"We must repair the error at once, or by all that's devilish, that girl will set him free," said the Boy Rover, as he entered the passage.

"Shouldn't be surprised, captain," remarked Jim, "if she hasn't been more wide awake than us, and done it afore now. Let a woman alone for having her wits about her."

"Curse her, if she has!" muttered the youthful captain; "for, in that case, we may have some tough work with him."

"Daresay we shall," remarked Ned, nudging his companion Jim in the ribs with his elbow, and leering round, as much as to intimate that he derived some slight pleasure at his captain's discomfort.

"At all events, he will not be able to do much damage," said the Rover, "as I have deprived him of his weapons; and there are none, I believe, in the cave that we need care much for."

"That was a rum go, that he should manage to lay hold of them," said Jim.

"Yes," remarked the other; "and confounded fortunate that he couldn't fire straight when he got them."

"Straight enough," said the Boy Rover, as he placed his hand to his grazed temple. "That shot was well meant, and nicely aimed. I have had a few escapes, but this was the most narrow one of all."

"Your time ain't come yet, captain" said Jim.

"No," he answered, in a somewhat thoughtful tone; "but the life we lead is so full of danger, that it may come at any moment. But, come when it will, it shall find the Boy Rover unflinching to the last."

It was the brutal courage of the Boy Captain that enabled him to hold with so firm a hand his crew of desperate ruffians in such admirable discipline, as we shall see anon; and his fearless disposition was held in the highest admiration by both Ned and Jim. In their ignorant natures, they mistook the desperate passions of the boy captain for the noble deeds of a hero; and the unflinching determination with which he followed out any pursuit, as the powerful force of the master's mind.

They feared him, for he inspired them with awe; they obeyed his every command, for they felt that any resistance to his orders would ensure their instant destruction; but not one of his desperate crew entertained for him the least respect. They would fight by his side, or shield him from harm at the sacrifice of their own lives; but yet they hated the man or boy—for such he was in years—hated him with an undying hatred: but still they dared not show it, for he possessed indeed the master mind of that hellish band; he was the greatest villain in that assembly of villains, and his fall would have been their irreparable ruin.

Had his course of life been different, still he would have been superior to his fellows. His was a mind that would have soared above the ordinary difficulties of life, and he would have gained position and success in any other channel.

Had the Boy Rover been started in life in an honourable path, the qualities of his mind would have raised him to a proud eminence, and he would have commanded the respect and admiration of honourable men as much as he now awed and enslaved his ruffianly crew.

It was, then, with blind obedience to his orders that Ned and Jim followed the Boy Rover along the passage to the cave.

It was with a light step the youthful captain entered the cavern; but scarce had he done so than, with a yell of rage, he bounded forward, like a wounded tiger, followed by his two companions.

CHAPTER VIII.

THE LOVERS—THE ROPE—THE ESCAPE FROM THE CAVE—A MOMENT OF HORROR.

WHEN the Boy Rover, accompanied by his myrmidons, Ned and Jim, left the cave, Ellen gave a sigh of relief, and allowed her head to fall on the shoulder of Charles Lawson, in which position she relieved her overburdened heart by a flood of tears.

The youth did not attempt to interrupt her; he felt that it would be far better to let her grief have full sway.

And in this he was wise; for, after the lapse of a few moments, she once more became calm.

Then she raised her head from the shoulder of her lover, and, fixing her large lustrous eyes upon his face, with a gaze half melancholy, half fearful, she said—

"Charles, it would seem that heaven had deserted us in this our terrible hour of need."

" Do not despair, Ellen," said the brave youth. "Hope for the best; hope on. If once we give way to despair we are lost."

"We are lost now, Charles—lost indeed!"

"Not so, Ellen. True, I am powerless, in my present position, either to aid you or to protect myself; but that villain, in the blindness of his passion, has forgotten that you are free to aid me."

"Would to heaven that I could!" replied Ellen.

"You can, dear one," said her lover.

"Oh! speak, Charles—now."

"Your hands are free, if mine are imprisoned. You can release me from these bonds," replied the young man.

"Oh, yes, yes," she exclaimed, eagerly. "Surely my poor brain must be turned, or I should have seen that before."

She seized the rope which bound the hands of the youthful lover, and essayed to untie the fastenings.

"There," she exclaimed, as she cast the cord upon the ground, "you are free. But," she added, as a look of pain overspread her beauteous countenance, "we are still prisoners."

"For a time," he replied, with a sickly smile. "I will not be taken by surprise again. We will escape from here, Ellen, if escape by any means be possible."

"Would to heaven that we could; but much I fear that even now the eyes of that fiend is upon us, watching our every movement, and waiting ready to spring upon us from yonder passage."

"Let him come, said Charles, as he cast his eyes around, in the hope of discovering some weapon wherewith to defend himself and his companion in misery from any attack—"let him come; he shall not gain so easy a victory this time. Can I but once get his throat in this grasp, he should feel that a British sailor can hold tight, whether his grip be to save his body from the foaming waves or a villain's power."

"But, Charles, his companions would avenge him. Surely we are sorely placed,"

"In truth we are, Ellen," he replied. "But he fears not to dare the winds and the waves, but not despair, when the whirlwind of misfortune encircles him. Fear not, Ellen; I will go to the passage, and listen if I can hear anything of them,"

"Oh, be careful!" she said, imploringly.

"For your sake, dear Ellen, will seek no unnecessary danger."

He stooped, and raised from the floor a small piece of wood which had lain there. It was the only thing he could see which he might be able to turn into a weapon of defence; and he resolved to use it, if need be.

He advanced to the passage listening intently.

Not a sound broke the stillness, and he was about to turn to Ellen's side, and bid her follow him, when the voice of Ned fell upon his ears.

He strained his eyes in the endeavour to catch a glimpse of the smuggler; but in this he was not successful. So he advanced silently a few paces into the passage, and again strained every nerve to overhear their conversation.

And in this he was successful.

Their words had little interest for him, but they proved to him that the passage was guarded, and that any attempt to escape by that direction was sure to lead to discovery.

He turned and entered the cave, where he found Ellen had followed him to the end of the passage, and was tremblingly awaiting his return.

He placed his finger on his lip to enjoin silence; then, taking her by the hand, led her back to the rude couch, and, seating himself beside her, said—

"Ellen, that passage is guarded. If we attempt to escape by that, we are sure to be discovered; yet we may succeed. We should have to contend with three desperate wretches, and the chances are we should again be overpowered; still I am willing for your sake to run the risk."

"It would be useless," replied the poor girl. "We should but fail; and then our sufferings, if possible, would be made more terrible. Oh! Charles, cannot there be some other means of flight?"

The youth paused ere he replied.

"I can see but one," he said, at length.

"What is it?" she inquired, eagerly.

"By the opening to the sea," he replied, pointing, as he spoke, to the partition through which they had looked upon the waves when the entrance of the Boy Rover surprised them.

The poor girl looked despairingly in his face.

"Then we are lost," she said.

Charles Lawson rose from her side as he exclaimed—

"Ellen, I am not unused to danger; but you have never had to encounter it till now.. You saw the waves leaping and foaming upon these rocks through yonder opening; you saw the depth from this accursed place to those billows; you saw the fearful danger that must attend my attempt to reach the water from here. I ascended to this place by means of a rope; but that rope was gone when I again looked for it. Still, if you have the courage to try it, I will secure some of these cords, and descend with you in my arms to the waves beneath, There lies our only hope of escape; and a poor one indeed it is. The waves may dash upon the rocks, and leave our mutilated bodies upon their rugged sides; or may carry us out into the wide expanse to perish. Will you escape by this means? Will you risk your life to the mercy of the waves, or wait, and trust to chance to release us from this horrible place, and the power of these ruthless monsters."

Ellen rose, and, throwing her arms around his neck, exclaimed—

"The waves will be more merciful to us, dear Charles, than the fiends into whose power we have fallen; for they but follow the dictates of the Almighty. To them, then, will I trust my body, and, with faith in heaven, dare the dangers that will beset us."

"Nobly and heroically spoken, Ellen. This base-hearted Rover shall find that there is a woman who dares meet death rather than dishonour; and a British sailor who will brave every peril to save the woman he loves."

He imprinted a kiss upon her lips, and, bidding her listen intently for any sound which should denote the return of the smugglers to the cave, he walked round the rude place, and selecting some pieces of rope from among the immense quantity strewed about, placed them on the board which had served as a table.

Then he gathered together, as silently as possible several planks. These he secured together by the ropes, till they formed, as it were, one piece. Then, fastening the end of a long rope, which he had laid aside from the rest, to the centre cord which bound the planks, he advanced to the partition, and drew it aside.

The bright moon shone full upon him, and revealed to his gaze the dancing waters beneath, and the rugged sides of the rock on which he stood.

He beckoned to Ellen, and in a moment she was at his side.

"Look forth," he exclaimed. "Does your courage fail you?"

"No," exclaimed the brave girl; "with you I will meet death in any form."

"'Tis well," he replied; and, returning to the rude table, he took the end of the rope in his hand, and returned to the opening.

"I must find some place to fasten this to," he said, as he cast his eyes about. "Ah," he added, suddenly placing his hand upon an uneven piece of the rock, at the side of the opening—"this will do; it would bear the weight of twenty."

Quickly he secured the rope to this; and then, laying his hand upon the arm of Ellen, he drew her back to the table.

"Help me," he whispered, "to get this timber to the mouth of this accursed place."

Silently they bore the planks to the opening; and then grasping the rope firmly in his hands, he pushed it out over the rock with his foot, and gradually let the rope run through his hands till the planks floated on the heaving billows.

Poor Ellen watched him with a heart beating between hope and fear.

"On that frail support, Ellen," he said, "we must trust ourselves. Are you still resolved?"

"I am," she answered.

"Come, then," he exclaimed—"place your arms around my neck. Cling to me, firmly, and fear not."

She threw her arms around his neck, and placed her beating heart against his manly breast. The young sailor grasped the rope firmly.

"Are you ready?" he asked.

"Yes," she replied, firmly.

"Come, then," he exclaimed, as he flung himself from the opening. "Come, Ellen; this rope leads us to liberty or death."

Down, down they went, over the side of the fearful rock. Below them the waves were rolling in the bright moonlight, and curling their foam-crested heads upwards towards the lovers, as they dangled in mid-air, as though they wooed them to their embrace. Down, down that slender cord, her arms encircling her lover's neck, and her head nestling upon his noble breast; down, down till the waves almost threw their silvery spray upon their forms. They had but a short distance now before they would reach the frail raft upon which they were to entrust themselves to the mercy of the boundless deep; a few yards more, and they have escaped from the power of the Boy Rover. Charles Lawson gazed upwards at the opening in the rock, and quickened his speed down the rope. A cry of horror would have escaped him, but he feared to alarm the poor girl, who reposed so confidently on his bosom. But a cold perspiration broke out upon his brow. In that glance upwards he had seen in the bright moonlight the demoniac features of the Boy Rover, gazing down upon him and his fair burden. He saw him draw his cutlass across the rope; he felt it twisting in his hand; and he allowed it to run through his fingers till they were almost torn to the bone. There was a sudden jerk, and he knew the rope was breaking. He let go his hold with one hand, and threw his arm around her form; and the next moment they were plunged violently upon the raft, which sank with them under the waves.

CHAPTER IX

THE CAVE DESERTED FOR THE SHIP—THE FRUITLESS SEARCH FOR THE ESCAPED.

BOUNDING forward, followed closely by Ned and Jim, the Boy Rover stood in the centre of the cave.

He cast one rapid glance around, and his eye rested upon the opening. In a moment he perceived that it was by this that his captives had escaped him.

He rushed to the opening, and his quick eye instantly detected the rope. Casting his eyes downward the bright moonlight revealed to his gaze the young lovers suspended half-way down the rock.

Maddened with rage, he grasped the rope with one hand, and drew the keen edge of his cutlass across it.

"Curse them!" he exclaimed, his cheeks livid with passion—curse them!" but they shall not escape. I will foil them yet. Never shall they escape to betray the secret of this cave. Ha, ha! down they go—to death, to death."

He watched the effect of his hellish work with foaming lips and blood-shot eyes; and his base cruel nature gloried in the act.

He saw those two young forms fall; he saw the waves close over them, and a fiendish smile wreathed his lips.

"There's an end to them both—curse them!" he exclaimed, turning to his followers, whose eyes had followed the young lovers till the waters shut them out from their sight, and who now turned their face to their captain, with a half-pitying look upon their countenances.

"Hard lines that, captain," said Jim. "They might just as well have never come ashore from the wreck of that ere craft."

"What a fool I must have been not to have known that the girl would release him if she got a chance! And you," he added, savagely, "even you had neither of you the sense to see it."

"Well," said Ned, in a nettled tone of voice, "if you didn't think of it, you couldn't expect us."

"It's no use being wild with us," remarked Jim. "If, instead of cutting the rope, we had all three caught hold of it, and hauled it up, why we should have got 'em back, safe and sound."

"Confusion!" said the captain, stamping his feet with rage. "My mad passion has foiled me. Why the devil couldn't you say so before I cut the rope?"

"Because you wouldn't give me time," was the reply. "But even now you may again get them in your power. They may float out to sea. The waves do not roll in so heavily now; and depend upon it the lad won't desert her while he can take a stroke."

"That fall has dashed them to pieces," said the captain, as he again looked out from the opening into the waves beneath.

"Don't think they fall very far," said Ned. "The rope went through his hands like lightning just before you severed it."

"Had we a boat at hand," said the Boy Rover, impatiently, "we might pick them up. But, curse it, not one is here because it is wanted. I can see nothing of them," he continued, "for that cloud that is now crossing the moon throws a gloom upon the waters. But they shall not escape me, if death has not already claimed them. Secure this opening, and we will away to the ship, and send off the boats to look for them. Curse them!—to be thus foiled; and at a time, too, when I felt so secure of the prey. Come!"

Ned and Jim closed and secured the wooden covering to the opening, which was used for the landing of the contraband goods from the boats, and followed the Boy Rover from the cave.

Emerging from the passage up into the open air, they lowered a large flat stone over the mouth of the entry, which effectually shut out all appearance of a cavity, and hurried away, along the rocks, in a southerly direction.

Chafing with rage and disappointment, the Boy Rover strode moodily on, followed by his two companions, for the distance of nearly a quarter of a mile. Then, turning the angle of a rock, the tall masts of a vessel were revealed to their view.

She was anchored in a narrow channel, between two high rocks, which effectually hid her from sight, either by land or sea.

This was the harbour of the "Venomed Snake," when gorged by contraband goods, or when it was found necessary to seek refuge from the revenue cutters, who were always on the look out for her.

They would oft chase her over the waves, and when almost assured of seeing her, would suddenly find she had disappeared, but where she had gone no one could tell.

Had they examined the coast more minutely they might have discovered her place of refuge; but from any distance the opening between the rocks was almost imperceptible; and when once within it, she was so effectually hidden, that those who eagerly sought to capture her believed it to be a phantom ship, and would turn the heads of their vessels seaward again, under the belief that they had been lured on by a mirage to a fruitless chase.

She was a plain fore and aft schooner, and a most mischievous-looking craft. There was not a line of rope in her beautiful tracery of rigging, spars, or hull that could possibly have been found fault with. Even the most experienced observer could not have failed to observe a peculiar beauty and mystery in her appearance. The heavy sails, and long narrow hull that upheld them, proved that she had been built more for speed than aught else.

A gleam of pride sparkled for a moment in the eyes of the Boy Rover, as they rested with the glance of an experienced sailor upon the fine graceful proportions of the noble craft.

Taking the small whistle from his breast, which he had used to summon the smuggler from the cave a short time previously, he blew a long shrill note. In a moment a sound similar to that which he himself produced floated from the vessel over the water, and echoed round the rocks.

Another minute, and a boat put off from the ship, and rapidly neared the spot on which the Boy Rover and his two companions stood.

Swiftly it glided over the waters that intervened between that gallant craft and the shore, and was suddenly and skilfully brought to a stand-still at the smuggler's feet.

The Boy Rover entered it, followed by his companions; and, waving his hand, the men bent to their oars, and the boat glided steadily from the rocks to the vessel's side.

Seizing a rope which hung from her bulwarks, the Boy Rover, with the agility of a cat, sprang from her side, and stood upon the deck.

In an instant he was followed by the others, and the boat secured to her stern.

A dark-featured young man appeared, and respectfully saluted him. This was Black Bill lieutenant of the "Venomed Snake." He was a thick-set broad-shouldered fellow, with muscles of iron, and a cast of countenance that bespoke a cruel and determined disposition.

"Have the boats manned," said the Boy Rover, addressing his lieutenant. "A girl, together with her lover, a young sailor, have but now escaped from the cave, by the opening to the sea. They may not have perished. See that every search is made, and every means adopted to secure them, if they have not paid for their daring courage with their life."

Black Bill made no reply, but saluting his captain, instantly gave the order to man the boats.

In a minute more the three boats belonging to the vessel were manned, and put off from the ship.

The Boy Rover leaned over the bulwarks, and gazed after them for some minutes. Then turning to his lieutenant, he said—

"Have you made all preparations for sea?"

"Your orders have been implicitly obeyed, captain," returned Black Bill, "and we but wait the command to weigh anchor."

"'Tis well," said the young captain. "As soon as the boats return, we will set sail."

"Whether they are successful or not," asked his lieutenant.

"Yes," was the reply. "You will give me notice of their return."

So saying, the Boy Rover turned and strode to his cabin.

One by one the boats returned to the ships, after the lapse of about half an hour; but neither of them could discover anything of the escaped lovers.

Black Bill reported to the Boy Rover the failure of the expedition; and, with a bitter imprecation at his disappointment, the youthful captain gave the order to weigh anchor, and stand out to sea.

As the first gray streaks of morning were breaking through the eastern clouds, the "Venomed Snake" stole silently from out the narrow channel between the rocks, and glided majestically over the dancing waves.

CHAPTER X.

AFLOAT ON THE OCEAN—THE BOY ROVER AND WILD MADGE.

OVER the waves, like a thing of life and joy, glided the "Venomed Snake," bearing upon the bosom of those boundless waters a crew of the most reckless ruffians that ever congregated together at one time.

Perhaps no vessel ever set sail with so young a complement of hands; for there was not on board this craft one whose age exceeded two-and-twenty years; and yet better sailors or brave men could not often be met with.

But there was not the cool heroic courage of the

noble sailor, who steers his vessel amid the dangers of the ocean, or spills his blood like water for the honour of the flag under which he fights, or the security of the homes and happiness of his native land. Theirs was the bravery of the savage, and the daring of the brute, whose untamed passions know no bounds.

While the handsome little craft swept majestically on her course, her white sail glimmering in the morning sun, the Boy Rover, wearied by the excitement of the night's adventure, had sought his cot; and when the sun was high up in the heavens, and the land was almost receded from sight, he again made his appearance on deck.

But, his whole demeanour and appearance had undergone a change. He had thrown off the garb of a fisherman, in which we have hitherto seen him, and was now attired as an officer of the navy.

A gold band encircled his cap; and attached to his belt was a sword, the handle of which was richly chased and studded. A pair of small pistols, also, were fixed at his waist; and from a small opening in the breast of his blue frock-coat the richly chased handle of a small dagger protruded.

An air of stern command now sat upon his brow, as silently he paced the deck, or moodily gazed across the ocean.

Black Bill anxiously followed every look and action of his superior; and when at last he leant over the taffrail, and, seeming lost in abstraction, gazed down upon the crested waves, as they broke upon the vessel's side, he remarked.

"The weather is cheerful, captain, after such a storm as last night. It was fortunate we were anchored in our little harbour; for the gale would have tried her timbers severely."

The Boy Rover looked up at the face of his companion as he replied:—

"She has stood worse gales than that; but, as you say, 'twas fortunate. But I had rather every plank in the hull gaped wide enough to ship a hundred seas than that she should now dance over foam without that girl on board."

"Cursed unfortunate," remarked Bill; "but, captain, that young fellow must have had more pluck in him than a good many to have risked life and limb to save her in the way he did. By Jove! if he should succeed in carrying her safe into port, he will earn her gratitude, and deserve her love."

The Boy Rover bit his lips in vexation as he replied.

"Fury seize him!—but for the carelessness of leaving that confounded rope dangling from the rock, he would never have found his way into the cave, and the girl now would have been securely in my power. They must not escape; they know the secret of the cave, and can bring destruction upon us. If they did not both meet their deaths when I cut the rope, they must have been carried out to sea."

"And, if they were," said Bill, "that fellow would hold on to her while a gasp of breath remained in his body."

"Ay," said the boy captain, "and a passing vessel might have rescued them both. Have you made out a sail?"

"Not a speck on the ocean, captain."

"And her course has been kept as I ordered?" asked the Boy Rover.

"To a point," replied the lieutenant.

"Then they must have perished," muttered the young man, thoughtfully.

"I can scarcely entertain a thought otherwise," replied Bill, "or we must, under ordinary circumstances, have run foul of them."

The Boy Rover remained abstractedly gazing over the wide expanse of waters for a few moments; then, suddenly raising his head, and addressing his lieutenant, he said:

"We will make a longer run this time. It would not be safe to return to the cave too soon; for if, by any chance in the world, they should fall in with a vessel, the cave would be in the hands of the Philistines, and there would doubtless be not a few to welcome us home."

"True," said Bill; "and as I, for one, have no wish to fall into their hands, a long voyage will be preferable; and even then it will be desirable to feel the coast a little before we land either ourselves or our cargo."

"See that the helmsman keeps her on her present course for some time," said the Boy Rover, after a pause; and then, casting another look over the undulating ocean, he turned away from his lieutenant and descended below.

There were two cabins; one devoted to the use of the Boy Rover; the other to that of a woman some forty years of age, and known on board the "Venomed Snake" by the name of Wild Madge.

Many and vain were the surmises of the smuggler crew as to who and what she was; and fruitless had hitherto been all their endeavours to discover what relation she bore to their captain.

To the rough crew of that schooner she was morose and silent, and seemed to inspire them with a kind of dread; and it would have been to many of them a feeling of relief had the boy captain not allowed her to sail with them. Still not one would have hazarded a remark to that effect to him.

Certain it was that there was some mysterious relation between them; for he, so rough and austere to them, was as gentle and kind as a child.

It was to the cabin occupied by this being that the Boy Rover now bent his steps.

Placing his hand upon the handle of the door he entered without ceremony, and, advancing to the centre of the apartment, stood face to face with Wild Madge, who rose from her seat at the table when he entered.

She was a woman of commanding stature, and had at one time been handsome; but now her features presented a bloated and besotted appearance. The once lustrous eye was dimmed by dissipation; and the once majestic carriage was now bent with over-indulgence to that most fatal of all vices—drink.

At the moment of the Boy Rover's entrance she held the glass containing brandy to her lips, and set it down upon the table as he advanced into the cabin.

"Well, Richard," she said, "you have not brought the bird on board which they told me you had trapped. Why did you trouble me to get everything in readiness for her had you intended to come alone?"

"I did not intend to come alone, mother;" he answered; "but the bird has escaped."

"Ha!—escaped, has she?" replied the woman in harsh vexed tones.

"Yes, for the present, at any rate."

"I am sorry for that," said Wild Madge, as she seated herself in the chair from which she rose at his entrance—"very sorry."

The Boy Rover fixed his eyes intently upon her countenance, as she gave utterance to these words, as though he would read there whether she truly meant them.

"Sorry," he iterated, "why should you be sorry?"

"Because," replied the woman, as her dim eyes lighted up with a momentary fire; there would have then been one as wretched as myself on board this bark."

"But that one," said the Rover, "would have been a woman—one of your own sex."

"Aye, and there would have been the joy," she replied.

"Mother," said the young man, as he gazed almost sternly into the bloated countenance of his companion, "are you sober, or are you mad that you should feel a pleasure in the misery of one of your own sex?"

"Boy," she exclaimed, as she rose from her seat and grasped his wrist "it may seem strange to you, that I—a woman—should exult in a woman's misery; but I tell you that your disappointment at the escape of this girl does not equal mine."

"Strange," said the youth, half-aloud, half to himself, "that a mother should feel a delight at her son's triumph over an innocent girl."

"Aye," said the woman, "strange to you, but not to me. Richard, look upon me. I was once fair and innocent, with a nature full of love and kindness; what am I now?—a foul blot on the name of woman. But who made me what I am? Woman!—therefore do I hate my sex. I was once happy, but a woman blighted that happiness. I loved with all a woman's gentle nature, but a woman's wiles turned that love to bitter hate. Woman has been the serpent in my path, whose venomed sting has pierced my soul and poisoned every better feeling—women's arts have curdled the milk of human kindness in my breast, have blasted my every hope, destroyed my every happiness, blighted my existence and made my life a living hell. This has woman done to me, and now a woman's wrongs and sufferings call for vengeance on woman's head, and gloat in woman's misery!"

Bad and dishonourable as was the nature of that youth he could scarcely help giving utterance to a feeling of disgust at these words.

For a moment or two he stood silently thinking. What wrongs must that woman whom he had called mother have endured he thought,to embitter her so fearfully against her sex. There could be no slight cause for this expression of illfeeling towards those who could have never wronged her; for surely the young girl whom he had intended to have brought on board his schooner could have never done her harm. Yet to that unfeeling woman it would have been a source of joy to have triumphed in her misery.

Suddenly he was aroused from the reverie into which he had fallen by Wild Madge thrusting a glass filled with brandy into his hand.

"Drink, Richard," she said; it will to some extent allay the pain of your disappointment. 'Tis the elixer of life. It will smooth your ruffled spirit as it drowns the bitter memory of the past. I should go mad Richard, but for this. When the wrongs I have suffered force themselves upon me with their overwhelming weight, I fly to this, and forget in its soothing influence the blighted hopes, the sufferings of years, the promised happiness, destined never to be fulfilled."

The Boy Rover dashed the glass aside, and its contents fell upon the floor of the cabin.

"I want not that," he said, "to fire my blood. Tis heated sufficiently by my natural passions,and requires not artificial aid."

"Wait till you know misery such as mine has

been," was the answer she made, as she refilled the glass,and poured its burning contents down her throat. "Ha, ha! it gives new life, as it sets the blood coursing through my veins. When my brain is fired by the fumes of this nerving liquor I feel equal to anything that may come."

"Would you but drink it less,"said her companion, in a tone of disgust, "you would become more a woman, and less a fiend."

"Oh, oh!" she laughed, derisively—"has the Boy Rover foresworn his calling? Has the oath he swore been forgotten? Has his once bold heart become nerveless?"

"Hold!" he exclaimed, savagely. "I am what I am—an outcast from society, a smuggler, and—"

"A murderer!" said the woman, with marked emphasis.

"Ay," said the Boy Rover, "a murderer."

A smile played round the lips of the woman as she emptied the glass again.

"And now you shrink from your own crimes?"

"No," he replied, "I am what fate has destined me to be, and what your teaching has engendered."

"Would you shrink now," she asked, "from avenging a mother's wrongs?"

"No," he exclaimed—"I have sworn to track to the death the villain who destroyed your happiness; for he has made me what I am."

"Ay, Richard, he has made us what we are—outcasts in the wide, wide world; the scorn and loathing of all the right-minded portion of humanity. Long ere this had death folded me in its icy embrace, but that I have sworn to live for vengeance; live to triumph in the misery of one who could feel no pity for me; live to make you, my boy, the instrument to insatiate vengeance. Oh! how my brain whirls when I think of the time when I shall gloat in his anguish; for it will come—ay, it will come!"

And again did she refill and empty the glass.

"Drink, boy," she said—"drink! Some there are who deny that brandy gives vigour to the frame. Ha, ha! did they but know how its fumes cheer my heart and fire my brain—how it gives strength to my determined resolves—they would say different. Were it not for this I should go mad. It drowns my sorrows, the bitter recollections of my past life, and urges me on to the gratification of my revenge. It will come, boy—it will come; and then this weak frame shall be made strong by agony; these dim eyes sparkle with joy at his sufferings—this withered heart bound with exultation at the misery that I will inflict upon him! Oh! how I long for the hour when he shall feel the vengeance of her whose love he scorned, whose life he embittered, whose honour he stole, and in whose misery he exulted. Drink!"

The Boy Rover took the proffered glass, and drank off its contents.

"There, mother," he said, as he handed the glass back to her—"are you satisfied?"

"Yes," she answered. "You will send me some more of this; for it is my greatest support. It is the only god that now I worship; for it stifles the bitter thoughts that at times rise to my heart, and is now the only medicine that will administer to this diseased heart."

There was a loud knock at the door of the cabin at this moment, and the Boy Rover placed his hand upon the latch and opened it.

Black Bill stood on the threshold.

"Captain," he said, "there's a sail coming up hand over hand."

THE PARTING OF THE RAFT.

"What do you make her out?" asked the Boy Rover.

"Looks all a cutter by the glass," was the reply.

"I will come on deck," said the young captain, "and see what I can make of her."

And, turning to Wild Madge, he remarked:

"I will be with you again;" then left the cabin, and returned to the deck with his lieutenant.

When the door of the cabin had closed behind him, Wild Madge sank back in her chair, and a smile stole over her blear countenance as she muttered to herself:

"It works! My teachings have not been in vain. I have instilled into his heart all the passions of a demon, and his soul is blackened in crime. But I must not rest here. No, no; he must become more hellish yet; his crimes must be greater, deeper, blacker! Would that I could induce him to drink more; then, under its fiery influence, he'd stop at nothing. Ha, ha! I shall yet mould him to my will; weave round him the web of crime so closely that escape will be impossible; ensnare him on to deeds so black that humanity shall stand appalled at the bare contemplation of them; and, when the time arrives, I, Wild Madge—mother as he calls me—will show myself to him in a form he has never dreamed of. But not yet; the time has not yet arrived. But it will come; and, when it does, I shall triumph; aye, triumph!"

4

And again did she swallow more of the fiery spirit; and then, leaning her arms upon the table, she buried her head upon them.

There was a hurried tramp of feet to and fro upon the deck; and the sound of hurried orders came upon her ears: but the fumes of the brandy were fast causing a drowsiness to steal over her senses; and in a few moments the deep heavy breathing showed that she slept.

But it was not the calm peaceful slumber of the mind, oppressed by the fatigue of honest toil. The brain still worked, and carried that diseased mind back to years gone by—back to the time when she was fair and happy, when the bright sunshine of peace shed a halo of love and joy around her; but, too soon, alas! to be dimmed by the murky haze of misery and crime.

CHAPTER XI.

THE FISHERMAN'S DAUGHTER—THE LIBERTINE AND HIS VICTIM—THE DOUBLE BIRTH—THE CHILDREN ON THE BEACH.

LET us, for a short time, go back eighteen years prior to the events related in the preceding chapters. Eighteen years! To the aged, as they look back, this space of time seems nothing. To the youth, as he looks forward to it, it seems an age. What thoughts, what aspiration, will not that space conjure up in his mind? What airy castles will he not build in his imagination? What joys will he not hope to realise in that time? Yet, when the days, weeks, and years have passed by, he looks back upon them with a sigh, and finds that all his fond imaginings have vanished, and left not a wrack behind, save the marks on Time's hour-glass, to tell him that life's sands are running swiftly out.

Eighteen years! The child becomes a man; the strong man sinks to the sear and yellow age: thousands have been ushered into the world, and thousands have taken their flight to eternity.

Still the sands run out. History records their passage; but all alike are powerless to stay their progress. Still they run—grain by grain; and so they will continue, till chaos comes again, and all things cease.

But what a change had passed over the life of Wild Madge in eighteen years. Then she was a happy laughing girl, of twenty years of age, with scarce a care upon her mind—hardly one dark shadow in her path. She was happy; for she loved—loved with all a woman's fond devotion, and trusted with all a woman's faith.

But, alas! that faith was too soon to be shaken; that happiness to be blighted; that joy to be turned to sorrow.

She trusted, and was deceived; and her fond devoted love was turned to bitter hatred.

She was the daughter of a poor, but honest, fisherman. Her mother had been lost to her when but an infant; and she had none to advise and guide her in her girlhood but her father. True, he strove to do all that would render her happy; for he loved his beautiful child with all a parent's love. But she needed a mother's guidance: and that, unfortunately for her after peace, Providence had denied her.

She knew that she was beautiful; and the homage paid to that beauty had made her vain and haughty: and those of her own sex, in the little fishing village in which herself and father resided, pained by her contemptuous bearing, held aloof from her; and thus she was left with none to whom she could confide, or seek council.

A short distance from the village was a noble old mansion, the proprietor and occupier of which was also the owner of the property on which she resided.

He was a gay dashing young man, of a warm-hearted generous disposition; but he had the misfortune to inherit a considerable amount of property before he well knew how to take care of it; and his youth and inexperience soon caused him to make acquaintances, and consider those his friends who might have been much better described as enemies.

But their flattery won upon his heart, and ere long they had moulded him to their desires. Naturally free, he became reckless, and soon he was the gayest libertine among them.

He saw Madge Lovegrove, the fisherman's pretty daughter, and, as he fastened his glance upon her features, he saw the blood mount to her temples, and the smile of pleasure beam in her eye.

With a libertine's quick perception, he saw that she was pleased at his notice of her, and he felt that it would be no difficult task to win her.

He resolved to try, and often, as if by accident, he threw himself in her path.

Madge was pleased at his condescension, and her vanity became the more unbearable.

She thought that she was weaving a web round the heart of the gay young gentleman that would draw his love to her, and she fancied that one day she would be the mistress of the broad lands that surrounded her humble dwelling.

Poor fool! Like the moth she was hovering around the flame that at last would consume her.

She knew that she was beautiful, even if she was poor; and she imagined that that beauty would make her the mistress of his affections.

The young libertine saw that he had but to praise her beauty and feed her pride. He poured the honied words into her ears, and she dwelt enraptured upon his tones.

He promised to make her his bride; to take her from her humble cottage to a home of splendour; to administer to her every wish; to live for her, and her only.

She listened, she believed, and she fell!

Fell, as many have fallen before, at the shrine of ambition, vanity, and pride.

The love that had warmed the heart of Joseph Hanfield now cooled, and the fond girl whose love he had so striven to gain was now thrown heedlessly aside.

Months rolled on, and the too confiding girl found when too late that all is not gold that glitters.

But she found, too, that she was about to become a mother; and her soul was wrung with anguish.

She begged, prayed of him to fulfil his promise of marrying her; implored him to save her from shame: but in vain.

He offered the means of leaving her native village, and hiding her shame some distance from those who knew her: but he quietly, yet firmly, told her that he could not, nay, would not, make her his wife.

He said their stations in life were too distant, and ridiculed the idea of marrying a poor fisherman's daughter.

His pride was too great to make that humble girl his equal; but his soul had not been clean enough to hold her purity unsullied.

In vain were all her prayers and entreaties; he was firm, cold, and determined.

And, with tearful eyes and aching heart, she returned to that home where peace and happiness had reigned for so many years; to that father whose kindly smile had always greeted her, and welcomed her with a loving kiss.

And there, in misery and despair, she prayed for God's curses on the head of him who had blighted her happiness.

It was but a few days after her interview with her seducer, that one young girl of the village, whom, in her haughty pride, she had disdained to hold converse with, but whose keen perception had seen through the intentions of the young libertine, with a true woman's nature, hoping to warn her of her danger, ere it was too late, told Madge that her lover was married; that he had been married some few weeks prior, in London; and that his young bride would arrive at that place in a few days.

Had a thunderbolt fallen upon her head, it could not have rendered her more paralysed than did these words.

At first she would not believe it; but when she reflected that he had been absent some time, and, likewise, that she had observed many alterations being undergone in the old mansion, she felt that it was too true; and, in an agony of mind almost bordering upon distraction, she flung herself upon the floor of the cottage, and gave vent to her feelings in agonised sobs.

She cursed her pride, her beauty, which had lured her to her ruin; she cursed the hour she was born, and her betrayer: and, in feelings of bitter jealousy, she cursed the woman who had won his love, and usurped her place, and swore a bitter oath never to rest till she had encompassed the destruction of them both.

So fondly had she loved; so fiercely now did she hate—with that bitter hatred that never slumbers! She felt that her peace of mind was gone for ever, and she resolved to embitter the happiness of him who had wronged her, and of her whom her jealous madness made her firmly believe had robbed her of his love.

She had sank upon that floor in the overwhelming anguish of a broken-hearted woman; but she arose from it with the cool, determined, undying hatred of a fiend.

She had resolved to prove that

"Earth hath no pang like love to hatred turned:—
Nor hell a fury like a woman scorned."

From that day Madge Lovegrove went about her ordinary duties as usual; was cheerful in her conversation with her father; was affable and sociable with the other village maidens.

But beneath this calm exterior raged a volcano ready to burst forth when the moment should arrive to fan its slumbering fires into furious flame.

No one, not even her father, suspected her fearful secret, and thus months flew by.

The new mistress had arrived at the hall, as the residence of Joseph Hanfield was styled, and her presence there had kept away from her husband his libertine companions.

He who had once been all life and gaiety, now became the quiet unassuming gentleman, attending to the requirements and comforts of his tenants, and superintending the renovating of his estate which of late had gone somewhat to rack.

One evening about seven months after his marriage he had accompanied his young wife to the beach, and was walking with her upon the sands, when he was accosted by the person who was attending to several of the improvements on his estate, and leaving his wife to enjoy the cool evening breeze, he accompanied the man to some portion of the place where he wished to have his advice before proceeding with the alteration.

The sun was sinking into the west and tinting the clouds with a golden hue, and throwing across the sea a stream of golden splendour: the air was soft and balmy, and the hum of the sea came musically entrancing to the ears of Mrs. Hanfield as she gazed upon the lovely scene lost in wonder and admiration.

Suddenly she returned to retrace her steps up the beach, when she was confronted by Madge.

There was a look upon the young girl's face of mingled pain and sorrow.

The kind heart of Mrs. Hanfield was touched, for, with a woman's quick perception, she saw that Madge was like herself soon to become a mother.

Kindly she spoke to her, and inquired if she was not well.

The soft tones of the kind-hearted woman fell upon the ears of Madge with a poisoned sound, for they brought to her heart all the slumbering and bitter hatred she felt for her who she believed had stolen from her the man to whom she had sacrificed herself.

She saw the state of the poor lady, and she felt the pain it would inflict upon her heart to tell her all.

She resolved to tell her, that she might gloat in the misery that revelation would inflict; she determined to poison her happiness, and make her as wretched as herself.

And she spoke.

With flushed cheek and heaving bosom, the young wife listened to the tale of wrong; and, with the gratification of a demon grasping his prey, Madge told her all.

And those two women separated on that sandy beach, with feelings in the heart of each better imagined than described.

Madge returned to her humble cot with feelings gratified at the misery she had planted in the young wife's breast; and Mrs. Hanfield walked slowly towards the hall, her heart a prey to bitter feelings of anguish, and her mind dwelling upon the thought of how she had been deceived in him to whom she had given her pure and holy love.

That night, lights flashed hither and thither in that large house, and servants were astir; whilst Mr. Hanfield sat listening intently in a room adjoining the wife's chamber for the sound that should proclaim the birth of his firstborn.

And on that same night, in the humble fisherman's dwelling, a small weak voice and a mother's sobs alone broke the stillness that reigned around.

As the gray mists of early dawn were rising from the earth, a figure, slowly and painfully, dragged itself from the fisherman's cot towards the beach. It bore in its arms a young infant; and, painfully and sadly, it dragged itself along the sands, till close to the water's edge.

The sea was rolling in as Madge (for she it was), after kissing the infant she carried in her arms, laid it on the sands at her feet.

Then, slowly and painfully, she returned by the

way she came towards the cottage, ever and anon pausing and looking behind at the poor babe within a few feet of the rolling billows.

She gained the door of her cottage, opened it, and entered; closed it after her, and sought her couch.

The next day, when the old fisherman returned to shore, he found his daughter too ill to leave her bed. He tried everything in his power to give her ease and restore her health; but the case was beyond his skill—it was beyond his power to minister to a mind diseased.

Never, for a moment, had he dreamed of the state of his daughter; therefore, all thoughts of the truth were far from his mind.

Madge had successfully concealed her secret from all, save that poor broken-hearted lady who had just given birth to a daughter at the hall, and the father of that child, and her son.

On a bed of down, and nestled warmly to its mother's breast, lay one; on the sandy beach, with the silvery spray of the rolling waves splashing over its tender form, lie the other: the offspring of one father, but two mothers.

Both had loved fondly, faithfully. One was bowed with grief; the other torn with revenge.

A fortnight passed, and health and strength was fast returning to those two beings who on the same night, and at the same hour, had given birth to their firstborn.

One sat, supported by pillows, in a gorgeously furnished chamber; the other stood gazing fixedly and revengefully upon that mansion which contained those she had sworn to doom to misery and despair.

The firmness of resolve was stamped upon her features, and the passions of hell were loosened in her breast.

She was there to strike the first blow in her fight of vengeance.

Stealthily she approached one of the windows, and laid her hand upon the sash. It yielded to her touch; she opened it, and entered. Noiselessly she strode across the room, out at its door, along the hall, and up the staircase, till she arrived at the room next to that in which Mrs. Hanfield was sitting.

This she entered. A small lamp shed its feeble rays around the apartment, and, by its light, she perceived on one side of the room a child's cot. Silently she stole towards it, and gazed at the calm peaceful face of a slumbering infant.

A hellish smile played around her mouth as she raised the babe from its resting place, and nestled it to her breast; then, as noiselessly as she entered, departed from the room, descended the stairs, passed out at the low window, and stood once more in the front of the house, with the still sleeping babe pressed to her bosom.

"Now," she muttered, between her clenched teeth —"now shall the serpent-sting of misery fester in your hearts; now will I be avenged!"

In another moment she had gone; and years elapsed ere she again visited the place of her happiness and her misery.

Nine years passed away, and her existence had almost been forgotten by the inhabitants of that little fishing village, when one fearful night whilst a storm was raging, and the wild waves lashed the beach, and the heavens belched forth their electric fires, she stood close to her once happy home gazing upon the warring elements, and watching the eager throng of villagers who deserted their firesides to render any assistance that might be needed on the coast.

Suddenly her eye rested upon one who stood some distance from the villagers, and she strode silently and stealthily towards him and stood by his side. As a bright flash of lightning illumined the earth and sea he turned; their glances met; they recognized each other, and spell-bound the seducer stood face to face with his victim.

A gleam of triumph lit up the face of Madge as her grasp fastened on his wrist, and she hissed into his ears threats of so fearful a nature towards himself and his wife, that the blood ran back cold to his heart.

He strove to tear himself from her presence, but she clung to him with a demon's clutch; and, goaded to madness by her taunts, he raised his arm and struck her to the earth, then darted hurriedly from the spot.

In a short time the storm abated, and one by one the villagers returned to their homes, and the beach was once more deserted by all save that prostrate woman and a little boy, who with tearful eyes endeavoured to arouse her by sobbing out the words—"mother—mother!"

She recovered, and, leaning on that boy's shoulder, she swore to track to the death that man who but now had struck her down and all connected with him, and implored that child to assist in her revenge; and down upon that sandy beach they knelt together, and swore never to rest in peace till they had hurled destruction, misery and shame upon her seducer!

Ere the sun rose in golden splendour over the earth, that woman leading the child by the hand departed from the spot, and went none knew whither.

CHAPTER XII.

ON THE RAFT—THE OPEN SEA—THE SEPARATION. ALONE ON THE DEEP.

BREATHLESS, exhausted, and nearly senseless, our hero and heroine, together with the hastily and rudely-constructed raft, rose to the surface of the waves:

Never for one instant had the brave youth released his hold either of that fair girl or the rope by which he had descended from the rock.

Fortunately it was that he had not done so, for it brought the raft to their rescue; as, doubtless, had he once sacrificed his grasp on the cord, the raft would have floated away, and left them alone in their now almost powerless condition to the tender mercy of the waves.

In his descent, so suddenly accelerated by the cutlass of the Boy Rover, he had struck his head against a projection of the rock, and it was only the sense of poor Ellen's danger that saved him from sinking into insensibility.

It was with no inconsiderable difficulty that he succeeded in obtaining a safe footing on the raft for himself and his beauteous companion, for the waves threatened every moment to dash it to pieces against the side of the rock.

They succeeded at last in placing themselves firmly upon the frail support, and drawing the rope which he had fastened to the raft from out of the water and coiling it at his feet, he clasped Ellen firmly with one arm, so as to prevent her being thrown into the sea by any obstacle which they might encounter, and which, as the moon's disc was now obscured by black clouds, they might dash against ere they were aware of its proximity.

A huge wave rolled in and bore them close upon the rocks, then rushing back with a hissing, roaring sound, carried them far out into the waste of waters.

And thus they sat upon those three or four pieces of timber, rudely spliced together, clinging to each other, and dreading lest every wave as it broke against the raft should sweep them from it and separate them again.

And thus, fearing for each other's safety, hoping with the morning's light to find help and succour, they sat with their arms entwined around each other's form, till morning broke over that wide expanse of waters, and they saw that they had left the land far, far away, in the distance.

The sun rose in all its gorgeous splendour, lighting up the dancing waves, and tinting their crested tops with the hues of burnished gold, and thowing their refulgent beams upon those two wretched beings who had trusted their lives to the mercy of the waves, which rolled and tossed on the bosom of that boundless and unfathomable waste of waters.

Poor Charles, in his descent from the rock, he had struck his head so violently, as we have before stated, that the faintness caused thereby, together with the fearful exertions and trials he had undergone during the last few hours, were fast luring him to insensibility.

Higher and higher rose the refulgent orb in the blue vault of heaven; warmer and warmer became the slanting beams, until its bright rays poured down with an almost intolerable heat upon the devoted heads of the lovers.

Their misery was now added to by the almost intolerable pangs of thirst which assailed them; and down into the cool depths of those waters did they gaze, with longing eyes. Their lips were parched, and their tongues clave to the dry roofs of their mouths; and, though nothing but water was to be seen around them, yet they dared not attempt to quench their thirst from the clear blue fluid, for well they knew that to drink of it was but to accellerate the pangs with which they were assailed.

Fearful was the intentness with which Charles Lawson strained his now bloodshot eyes over that waste of waters, in the hopes of seeing the white sails of some vessel that might come to their rescue. But not a speck was to be seen on the ocean; nothing but the white crested waves met his sight on every side, and the blue expanse of sky above.

He gazed into the face of the fair being who sat silently by his side, and a heavy sigh rose to his breast as he saw there the misery she was suffering in silence and resignation.

On they went, carried by the winds and waves over the broad ocean, while the sun streamed upon their fevered brow, and burnt into their very flesh.

Still, silently and uncomplainingly, they gazed across the ocean for succour.

It was about mid-day, and when the sun was high in the heavens, and its fierce beams pierced their brains like molten lead, that Charles descried a small object in the sea drifting towards them.

He leant over the side of the raft, and watched it as it came nearer. He soon perceived it to be a small cask, and his heart beat with renewed hope as he thought it might perhaps contain something wherewith they might quench the thirst which consumed them.

Earnestly did he pray that it might drift within his reach; and that prayer was answered, for a wave bore the cask close up to the side of the raft; and, stretching forth his hand, Charles grasped it firmly, and drew it on to the raft: but, to their disappointment, they discovered it was empty.

The hopes that had risen in their breasts now sunk lower and deeper in their hearts; and, with pale cheeks and fevered brows, they again turned their anxious gaze upon the ocean.

A long branch of some huge tree drifted alongside their raft, and Charles instantly secured it.

"Ellen," he said, "have you a handkerchief?"

"Yes," replied the poor girl, as, placing her hand in the pocket of her dress, she drew it forth, and held it towards him.

"I will secure this branch to our raft," he said; "and your handkerchief, fluttering in the breeze, may be seen by some vessel."

"Heaven grant it may," she exclaimed; for, if we are not rescued soon, I fear I shall die of thirst."

"God forbid!" exclaimed the noble-hearted youth, as he pressed her hand, and gazed tenderly and pityingly in her face. Surely Heaven will send us succour soon."

Tying the handkerchief to one end of the branch, he secured it to the raft, in the hope that it might be instrumental in bringing some passing vessel to their rescue; and they once more resigned themselves to their fate.

The burning rays of the sun now streamed down upon them with an intensity that scorched the flesh, and almost penetrated the brain; for, having no coverings for their heads, they could in no way shield them from its fierce power.

The exertions and trials he had undergone, together with the oppressive heat, the intolerable thirst, and the sickening pain from the blow on his temples, was fast drawing to a state of insensibility the brave young sailor who had so nobly struggled for the sake of his fair companion.

Gradually his head sunk upon his breast, in spite of all his efforts to shake off the drowsiness that was now stealing over him: his eyes closed, his limbs became rigid, and he fell forward upon the raft, insensible.

With a cry of despair, Ellen knelt down by his side, and endeavoured to restore him to consciousness—but in vain; and, burying her face in her hands, the scalding tears chased each other rapidly down her cheeks, while heavy sobs shook her frame, and her bosom swelled with the powerful emotions that heaved within her breast.

And thus the time flew by, till, raising her head to gaze once more across the ocean, she uttered a wild piercing shriek, and started to her feet.

The rope that had bound together the boards which formed the raft had become loose, and the planks were fast parting asunder.

She seized the rope, and strained every nerve and muscle to draw them together again, and secure them as before; but all in vain. The waves dashed up between the separating planks, and forced them further and further apart, till they left a huge gap between the portion on which her lover lay and that on which she herself stood.

In an agony of despair, she exerted all her strength to keep them from parting. Frantically, she strained every nerve upon that rope; but the waves dashed in between the planks, and forced them wider and wider asunder; and the spray splashed up in her face, and almost blinded her, whilst the waters swept over the planks, threatening every moment to carry the insensible youth from his frail support, down into their clear blue depths.

Who can pourtray the agony of that poor girl, as she perceived the planks parting wider and wider from each other, and found that all the strength she could bring to bear upon the rope was insufficient to keep them together!

Fiercely, madly, did she strain every nerve; but all to no avail. Further and further they parted—greater became the gap between them every instant—and higher and stronger dashed the water through the opening; and, the planks slipping from the only fastening which held them together at one end, the rope suddenly slackened, and she fell backwards, as though struck by some sudden agency.

So fierce was the shock caused by her bearing her whole strength upon the rope, that, for a few moments, she was rendered powerless, and almost insensible; but the fearful danger with which she was surrounded, the horror of the situation, and the despair which assailed her heart for the fate of her noble-minded lover, roused her to consciousness, and, half-bewildered, she gazed around her.

That portion of the raft on which her lover lay insensible had drifted some distance from the planks on which she sat, and every moment the space between them became greater and greater.

She saw the waves curling their crested tops over its sides; and every fresh billow, as it rolled towards it, threatened to hurl him from the frail support on which his body was borne over the dancing waters.

Not one thought for herself—not one care for her own perilous position—her whole mind was centred on him, and on him alone.

Never for a moment did her eyes wander from that loved form as it rose and fell upon the waves, and was carried hither and thither across the bosom of the boundless deep.

She was saturated by the salt spray as it dashed high up over her fair form, but she heeded it not; felt not the briny waves as they beat over her, and leapt and danced and sported in the bright sunlight, as if revelling in her misery, and in mad glee mocking her sufferings.

Further and further became the distance between them, and the sight of the poor girl became weaker and weaker as she strained her eyes through the bright sunbeams over the waves towards that loved object whom she now believed was lost to her for ever.

The waters danced and curled as though they strove to hide him from her view: a mist stole over her eyes and giddiness seized upon her brain; she closed her eyes for a moment, and when she opened them again, she could discern nothing but the sparkling waters as they rolled around her, and curled their crested tops over each other.

Now, and now only, did she fully realize the horror of her own situation. She felt that she was alone—alone upon that wild waste of waters—alone upon the deep and boundless sea, without one near her on whom she could gaze, without one hand to aid her, without food or water to moisten her parched lips—alone, with a single plank only between her and eternity, with the bright blue heavens above her head, and the dark green sea beneath her feet, and bounded on every side by the foaming ocean—alone in her agony and wretchedness—alone, to die in madness and despair!

She clasped her hands and raised her eyes to the clear blue vault of heaven; but, as though to enhance her sufferings, the burning rays of the noon-day sun streamed fiercely upon her upturned features, and scorched the lovely face that pleadingly gazed upwards for aid.

Gradually the heavens and the sea faded from her sight; the sound of the rolling waters died away in a low melancholy moan; her head sank upon her breast; her arms fell powerless by her side, and she became unconscious to all her misery, while the planks on which she lay glided over the bosom of the boundless deep.

CHAPTER XIII.

THE REVENUE CUTTER—THE DEJECTED OFFICER—AN OLD SAILOR'S COURTSHIP—LOVE AND DISAPPOINTMENT—THE SPECK ON THE SEA—THE RESCUE OF ELLEN—RECOGNITION AND DESPAIR.

OVER the sea, her white sail glistening in the bright sunlight, with every stitch of canvas that she could carry stretched to its utmost tension by the breeze, and with the proud union jack fluttering from her mast, sped the noble little revenue cutter, the "Flying Dart."

She was a well-built and well-armed little craft, and carried five-and-twenty as brave British sailors as ever trod the deck of an English vessel.

She had been for some time past on the lookout for the smuggler, and though her crew had several times sighted the sails of the "Venomed Snake," yet they had never been able to come up with her ere she had mysteriously disappeared.

But from information her captain had received he believed he was now upon the track of that daring smuggler, and he sincerely hoped that ere the sun went down himself and his crew might have a chance of overhauling the smuggler's vessel, and carrying him and his unprincipled crew into port as prisoners.

The crew of the "Flying Dart" were also in high spirits at the prospect of a brush with the Boy Rover, and the prize money which would fall to their share should they succeed in making him strike his flag.

But they knew not the desperate natures of that youthful band of marauders, nor their numbers, or means of defence: had they been acquainted with this they would not have been so sanguine of success.

But hope ever comes uppermost in the mind of the British seaman. With the utmost faith in the skill of his commanders, with the certainty of his messmates' bravery, and the knowledge of his own unflinching courage, together with the influence that the unstained flag under which he fights throws over all, he always looks for victory, never for defeat.

Captain Waters, a noble specimen of a British officer, stood upon the quarter-deck, ever and anon raising his glass to his eye, and scanning with a seaman's glance the surrounding ocean.

Leaning over the tafrail, and gazing abstractedly upon the waves, as they leaped and sported around the vessel, was a young man, in the garb of an officer. He was the second in command on board the cutter, and was much beloved by his crew, and esteemed by his captain.

He had stood thus lost in thought for some time, and several times had the eyes of Captain Waters been fixed almost pityingly upon him.

After a long survey through his glass, in the hopes of discovering some sign of the smuggler vessel, Captain Waters approached the side of his lieutenant, and laid his hand upon his shoulder.

The young man started, and looked up in his commander's face.

"Mr. Chambers," said the captain, in a half bantering tone, "you do not expect to see the smuggler sail along under our bows, that you so intently fix your gaze there? Or," he added, as he saw the blood rush to the young man's temples, "is it the face of your lady love you imagine reflected on the waters beneath us?"

"I beg your pardon, sir," stammered out the young lieutenant, in a confused tone—"my mind was wandering, and for the moment duty was forgotten."

A smile stole over the face of the captain, as he remarked:

"By Neptune! Mr. Chambers, this must be the swiftest sailer afloat; for she has run eight or ten knots in the moment."

Lieutenant Chambers looked hard in the face of Captain Waters, as though he could not understand the meaning of his words; but the next moment a smile broke over his face, and he knew that the reverie into which he had fallen had been of some duration.

"I have been somewhat inattentive," he said, after a pause; "but I trust my temporary abstraction has in no way interfered with the calls of duty?"

"In this instance—no," replied Captain Waters, good naturedly. But so deeply were you lost in thought, that I verily believe a gun fired over our bows would have failed to rouse you."

"Then I must have been abstracted indeed, sir."

"And indeed you were," said the captain. "In fact, Mr. Chambers, I have perceived that of late you are subject to these moody fits. I trust that you are not unwell."

"No, sir, thank heaven, my health is good."

"Yes," interrupted Captain Waters, "but this may be no disease of the body, but of the mind."

And his glance rested upon the countenance of the young man as though he would read in his features the answer to his surmise.

A crimson flush overspread the temples of the young officer as he replied:

"I know of no ill that can assail my mind, sir."

"Humph!" exclaimed the other; "are you sure it is not the eyes and cheeks of that pretty girl we met at Mr. Hanfield's when we went ashore at Gibraltar, six months ago. By my faith, I think Cupid planted his dart in your bosom there, for ever since you have been as dull as a girl in the sulks."

The young man looked confused, and seemed lost how to make any reply. At length he stammered out—

"Miss Hanfield is very beautiful, certainly, and I—"

"Like a true British sailor, fell over head and ears in love with her," interrupted Captain Waters. "Is it not so."

"I—I, certainly——" stammered out the lieutenant.

"There, there," again interrupted the captain, as he saw the young man was both pained and confused by his badinage; "never mind," he added, extending his hand to the young sailor good naturedly; "if my remarks have pained you I am sorry for it. Why, you are not the first man that has nearly lost his senses through a woman. Why, Mr. Chambers, when I was your age, I nearly went stark-staring raving mad;

got myself into innumerable scrapes, and stood a very fair chance of making a too intimate acquaintance with an ounce of lead, and all through a pretty girl to whom I set sail and gave chase."

"And did you succeed in capturing her?" said the lieutenant, smiling, and pleased at the turn the conversation had taken.

"Not till after a smart chase," replied the captain; "you see, Mr. Chambers, there was another craft alongside, and so I had to manœuvre a bit, I can tell you to cut him out; and I found it no easy work, for so sooner did I make a little headway than down he bears broadside abeam of me, and tries to get on the weather gage, and then in disgust at both of us, the prize we both wished to take would make all sail on another course, and leave us to shew our teeth to each other."

"But how did it all end, sir, at last?" asked the young lieutenant, smiling at the captain's odd way of comparing a woman with a ship.

"Why, I chased her into a channel at last, where she could not easily escape; and there I succeeded in capturing and bringing her to anchor in the port of matrimony."

"But how about your rival, sir?" asked the other.

"Why, he had to strike his colours, to be sure. But, like a brave foe, when he found that I had fairly won the prize, he gave in with a good grace, and has been ever since one of my warmest friends. So you see, Mr. Chambers, I have been in love—happy and miserable at the same time: but it all turned out right at last."

"But you, sir, were the favoured suitor," said the lieutenant, and a sigh rose to his lips.

"And so may you be," returned the other, as he heard the sigh—"so may you be, sir; for it would puzzle Old Nick himself to know which way a woman's mind steers when she takes it into her head to be obstinate. Believe me, its no use being miserable about a woman because she won't confess that you, and you only, hold possession of her heart. They will play with a man as a cat does with a mouse, before they kill it. But, then, with woman, it generally ends by your being torn to pieces by love and kindness; and that will be your fate at last."

"I fear not," murmured the young man.

"Then it is as I thought, eh?" said the good-natured captain, smiling.

The young lieutenant started, as he discovered that he had involuntarily betrayed his secret.

But, having gone thus far, he determined to make his captain his confident, and he said:

"Well, sir, in truth, I was thinking of Miss Hanfield, when you placed your hand upon my shoulder and roused me from the reverie into which I had fallen."

"I thought so!" exclaimed Captain Waters.

"But why my mind should dwell upon her I can scarcely imagine," said the young man, "since she can never be to me more than an esteemed and valued friend."

"Then you are not in love with her?" queried the captain of the cutter.

"She loves another," said the young man, and again a sigh forced its way from his bosom.

"How do you know that?" asked the other. "Do you fancy, because after an acquaintance of a few months she does not fall into your arms, that you are indifferent to her?"

"No, sir; nor should I esteem much the love so lightly bought. But she loves another; thus much have I learned from her own lips."

"Whew! that's how the cat jumps. Then endeavour to forget her."

"That is impossible," returned the young lieutenant. "I saw, and I loved her; and, though the love can never be returned, yet I shall ever cherish the image in my heart."

The brave captain looked almost pityingly upon the youth at his side. He saw how deep that love had sunk in his breast; and he dreaded lest the disappointment should blight and embitter the existence of one who bid so fair to become one of the bravest and most daring officers that ever trod the planks of a ship that floated under the Union Jack.

He almost regretted that he had spoken to the youth on the subject; but, having done so, he resolved to leave no means untried to soothe his disappointment, and instil into his mind a conviction that it was unworthy a brave man to be so cast down because he had failed in winning the love of one on whom he had centred all his affections.

"I must keep him to his duty," he thought to himself; "leave him no time to think; keep his mind always employed on one thing or another; and then time will do the rest. He is brave as a lion, and strong as a fortress, and yet a woman's smile has broken him. 'Tis sad, very sad!"

And the good-natured captain paced the quarterdeck of his little craft in deep thought; and Henry Chambers once more leant over the tafrail and gazed into the sea.

It was at this moment that the look-out at the mast-head fancied he could discern some object floating on the top of the waves, a long distance from the ship, on her larboard bow.

Shading his eyes with his hand, he gazed intently, and endeavoured to make out what it could possibly be.

But in this he was unsuccessful. He could see something; but what that something was he could not tell. It might be a portion of a wreck—something thrown overboard to lighten a vessel in the last night's storm—or even a human being. So, hailing the deck, he called the attention of those below to it.

The captain raised his glass, and gazed in the direction indicated by the look-out; but failed to make out what it was.

"Take my glass, Mr. Chambers," he said, turning to the lieutenant, and handing him the telescope, "and see what you can make it out to be."

The young man took the glass, and gazed long and anxiously: then, suddenly lowering it, he said:

"It appears like the dead body of a woman floating on the waves."

Again the captain took the glass and centred his gaze upon the spot.

"I fear you are right, Mr. Chambers," he said, as he lowered the glass. "Have the ship laid-to, a boat lowered, and take the command of her. Heaven knows life may yet be not extinct, and doubtless it is some poor wretch who was wrecked in the storm of last night."

The order to lower a boat was instantly and cheerfully complied with, and in a very short time it was manned and gliding over the waves, with Lieut. Chambers setting its stern sheets.

Willing hands plied the oars, and leapt through the waters like a thing of life.

Captain Waters stood leaning over the bulwarks watching the receding boat, and wondering what had been the misery endured by that form floating in the sea, ere it had been cast upon the pitiless mercy of the waves.

And as he gazed after the small boat, a mere speck on that waste of waters, strange thoughts took possession of his mind.

"What might be his fate and the fate of his gallant crew? A storm might rise at any moment and his gallant little ship be dashed to pieces; she might strike upon some hidden rock, or a thousand other fates befall her; he might be cast to the mercy of those waves or buried beneath their rolling bosom, without one kind friend to sooth the last agonies of death—without one prayer to accompany his soul to eternity."

And as he thought his heart grew sad, and involuntarily he murmured a prayer to heaven for the safety of himself and crew; for though the bright sunlight of heaven now shown with all its sparkling glory upon the peaceful ocean, dark storms ere long might rise, and that world of waters lashed to fury by the howling winds, might engulph his devoted ship and crew in one fell vortex of destruction and death.

Eagerly, almost impatiently, did he watch the course of the boat, as it dashed over the waves on its mission of mercy.

And the crew, standing in knots of twos and threes, shading their eyes with their hands from the sun's rays, followed the boat's course, and speculated upon the object it would encounter.

With willing hands and willing hearts, the rowers pulled the little bark over the waters, cheered on by their much-loved lieutenant.

A heavy load seemed to have settled at the breast of the young officer—a load which he could not shake off, and for which he could not account.

He had been dull, nay, almost miserable, on board the ship; but now he was oppressed with some dismal foreboding for which he could not account.

He endeavoured to shake it off, but he could not succeed in doing so. There it sat, like some huge nightmare on his heart, and held him under its powerful influence.

Sailors are proverbially superstitious, and superstition reigned predominant in the breast of Henry Chambers.

He felt that he was going after something which was connected with his own destiny, and he believed that the object he was now so rapidly nearing would influence his life for good or for evil. Why, he knew not; but he felt it was so; and that feeling was rooted deeply in his heart.

"Pull, men — pull!" he said, addressing the rowers; "bend to your oars with a will!"

"Aye, aye, sir," responded the seamen, as they bent forward; and thus, bending themselves back, the boat shot through the water like an arrow.

"That's right," he exclaimed, as the long steady strokes of the oars brought them nearer and nearer every moment to the object they had descried from the ship. "Well done, lads! Now she glides through the water like a dolphin. Now, all together!"

And thus, urging on his men to renewed exertion, and ever and anon sinking into a train of thought, only to raise his eyes and find himself much nearer the object they had in view, they had placed a very considerable distance between themselve and their cutter.

The sea was now comparatively calm. The mad waves, which, a few hours before, had rolled so furiously, had now lost much of their vigour, and rolled more gently.

Had it been otherwise, Henry Chambers had not been sent on his errand of mercy, and one, at least, of our principal characters had met with an untimely fate.

CPSIA information can be obtained
at www.ICGtesting.com
Printed in the USA
BVOW04s0840040417
480259BV00008B/85/P